Primary Science for the Caribbean

A Process Approach

Book 4

Raphael Douglass   Trevor Garcia

TEC Sep 1999

Heinemann Educational Publishers
Halley Court, Jordan Hill, Oxford OX2 8EJ
A Division of Reed Educational & Professional Publishing Limited

OXFORD   MELBOURNE   AUCKLAND
JOHANNESBURG   BLANTYRE   GABORONE
IBADAN   PORTSMOUTH (NH) USA   CHICAGO

© Raphael Douglass and Trevor Garcia 1997

First published by Heinemann Educational Publishers in 1997

The right of Raphael Douglass and Trevor Garcia to be identified as the authors of this work has been asserted by them in accordance with the Copyright, Designs and Patents Act 1988.

British Library Cataloguing in Publication Data
A catalogue record for this book is available from the British Library.

Cover photograph by Roger Belix (Trinidad and Tobago)

Text and cover design by Gabriele Kern

Illustrations by Art Construction and B. L. Kearley Ltd

ISBN 0 435 04344 7

Produced by **AMR** Ltd

Printed and bound in Great Britain by Scotprint

00 01 10 9

Publisher's acknowledgements

The publisher would like to thank Mrs Sitara Gardner of the Ministry of Education for her advice and contribution to this book.

Authors' acknowledgements

Raphael Douglass would like to thank Mr Gordon Besson and Miss Joanne Debasee of NIHERST, Mrs Sharon Mangroo and Miss Althea Maund of the Curriculum Department of the Ministry of Education, and all the teachers who have been involved in trials of the activities, as well as making and testing his low-cost apparatus. He would also like to thank his daughter, Darlene, for her help on the series, and his wife, Lucille, for all the help and inspiration she has given him. Trevor Garcia would like to thank his wife, Lucy, for all her help and support with his work on this series.

Note to the teacher

To help you prepare for each lesson, you should read through the objectives and the pupils' text before each lesson. You should also refer to the Teacher's Guide, *How to Teach Primary Science for the Caribbean – New Edition*, which gives extra notes on certain activities and instructions on how to make equipment. We suggest that pupils work in groups where possible (see the Teacher's Guide for guidance). 'Your group will need' lists the equipment needed to set up each activity. Remember to multiply the materials listed according to the number of groups or individuals doing the activity.

Key words are in **bold** and explained in the text. There is also a glossary which lists some difficult words.

Contents

Chapter 1 Topic 1	**Clouds** (4 periods)		4
Chapter 2 Topic 2	**Air Pollution** (2 periods)		10
Chapter 3 Topic 3	**What Growing Plants Need** (4 periods)		14
Chapter 4 Topic 4	**Eyes for Seeing** (4 periods)		19
Chapter 5 Topic 5	**Thermometers** (3 periods)		25
Chapter 6 Topic 6	**Making a Balance** (3 periods)		30
Chapter 7 Topic 7	**Measuring Forces with Springs** (4 periods)		34
Chapter 8 Topic 8	**Separating Materials from Mixtures** (4 periods)		39
Chapter 9 Topic 9	**Floating and Sinking** (5 periods)		43
Chapter 10 Topic 10	**An Aquarium** (1 period)		49
Chapter 11 Topic 11	**Seeds and Leaves** (2 periods)		52
Chapter 12 Topic 12	**A Trip to the Beach** (3 periods)		56
Chapter 13 Topic 13	**Solid, Liquid, Gas** (3 periods)		62
Chapter 14 Topic 14	**Project Clean-up** (4 periods)		67
Chapter 15 Topic 15	**Life Cycles** (2 periods)		70
Chapter 16 Topic 16	**Bar Graphs** (4 periods)		76
Chapter 17 Topic 17	**Food Chains** (6 periods)		80
Chapter 18 Topic 18	**Which Aeroplane Flies Best?** (2 periods)		84
Chapter 19 Topic 19	**Concealed Objects** (2 periods)		88
Chapter 20 Topic 20	**Using Graphs** (3 periods)		90
Revision Test			94
Glossary			96

Note: The topic and period numbers refer to the Primary Science Syllabus for Trinidad and Tobago (1994).

Chapter 1 Observing
Clouds

There is water in the air, in the form of **water vapour**. Water vapour is a gas. It is formed when water **evaporates**. Hot air holds more water vapour than cold air. When air cools, water vapour comes out of it and forms water. We say that water vapour **condenses** when it changes back to water.

Bring materials to class when asked

Activity 1 Getting water out of air

Your group will need:
- 1 clear plastic container
- 3 ice cubes

Safety!
- Do not hold the ice cubes in your hand for too long.

1. Place the ice cubes in the container. Observe carefully.
2. Discuss what you see happening.
3. What do you notice forming on the outside of the glass?
4. Where does the water formed on the outside of the glass come from?

ice

Objectives
At the end of the chapter, pupils should be able to:
- describe how clouds form (pages 4–6).
- recognise fair weather clouds and rain clouds (pages 6–8).
- identify and name three different types of cloud forms seen in the sky (pages 6–8).

4

Observing

Activity 2 Making clouds and rain

Your group will need:
- a clear plastic container
- some clean gravel
- some hot water (about 50 °C), provided by your teacher
- 6 ice cubes
- 2 pieces of foil
- cotton wool

Safety!
- The hot water must be poured into the container by the teacher. Make sure your container is standing firmly on your desk when the teacher pours the water.

1. Put the gravel into the container so that it is higher at one side.
2. Shape one piece of foil into a bowl that just fits into the top of your container. Place the ice cubes in the foil bowl.
3. Make another foil bowl the same size. Fill it with cotton wool.
4. Ask your teacher to pour some hot water into your model. Now you have some land and a pond!
5. Quickly put the bowl with the ice on top of the container. Put the cotton wool bowl upside down on top of it.
6. Observe carefully. Discuss what you see with your group. Write down what you see in your notebook.

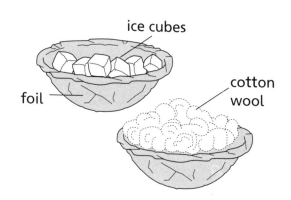

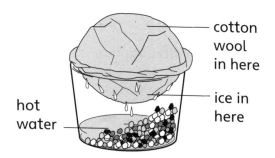

5

Observing

7 Copy and complete this table:

Cloud formation in our model	Cloud formation in the sky
a Hot water in the model pond forms water vapour (gas) at the surface of the pond.	**a** Water in rivers, ponds and the sea is heated by the _____ and forms water vapour (gas) at the water surfaces.
b Water vapour rises and condenses on the _____ surface of the foil. It forms tiny water droplets.	**b** Water vapour rises and _____ on the cold surfaces of tiny dust particles in the air. It forms tiny water droplets.
c We see all the tiny droplets together as a _____.	**c** We see all the tiny droplets together as a _____.
d The tiny droplets of water run into each other and join up together. They become _____ and heavier and fall as 'rain'.	**d** The tiny droplets of water run into each other and join up to each other. They become larger and _____ and fall as _____.

Water that falls out of the air as rain or snow is called **precipitation**.

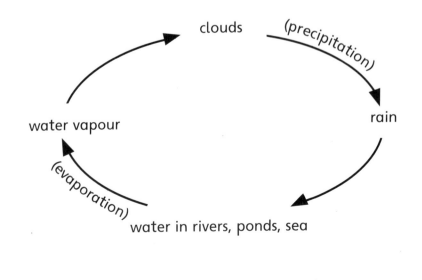

6

Observing

Activity 3 Looking at the clouds

1. Go outside with your group. Look at the clouds in the sky. Discuss the different shapes, the colour and the movements of the clouds you observe. Are they high up in the sky or quite low?
2. Are the high clouds and the low clouds different?
3. Is it hot or cold where the clouds are?
4. Do you think there are dust particles high up in the air? How did they get there?

Share knowledge with your group

5. Look at these cloud shapes and their names:

cumulus

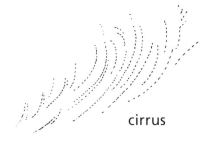

cirrus

stratus

Did you see any clouds like these? Go outside and look at the clouds again.

6. Draw the clouds you saw in the sky. Make a table like this:

Clouds in sky (draw what you see)	Name of cloud	High / middle / low

7

Observing

Cumulus clouds look like cotton wool at the top. They have flat bases. They are low clouds. They do not cover the whole sky. Lots of small cumulus clouds in the sky mean that the weather will stay fine.

When a cumulus cloud is tall and dark, and the top is shaped like an anvil, expect bad weather! There could be thunder and lightning.

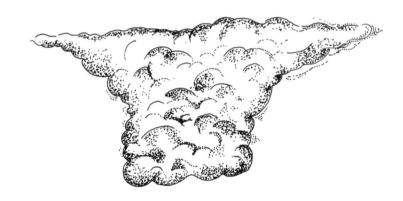

Stratus clouds form layers. They are low clouds. When they are dark as well, they could bring rain.

Cirrus clouds look feathery. They have jagged edges. They are high clouds. Cirrus clouds are so high that tiny ice crystals form instead of tiny water droplets. They are usually fair weather clouds.

Summary
- When water vapour in the air gets cold, it condenses into water droplets.
- The water droplets together make clouds.
- Small, white, fluffy cumulus clouds mean fair weather.
- Tall, dark cumulus clouds mean stormy weather.
- Stratus clouds are low clouds. They form layers.
- Cirrus clouds are high, feathery clouds.

Observing

Test yourself

For each task, write down **A**, **B**, **C** or **D**.

1 Clouds form in the sky when

   A water vapour condenses on cold dust particles
   B rain is about to fall   **C** water evaporates
   D the sky is not blue

   (Objective 1)

2 Michael and Carissa argued about types of clouds.
  Michael said dark low clouds are rain clouds.
  Carissa said cirrus clouds high in the sky seldom bring rain.

   A Only Michael is correct
   B Only Carissa is correct
   C Neither Michael nor Carissa is correct
   D Both Michael and Carissa are correct

   (Objective 2)

3 Clouds that are formed high in the sky are the

   A cirrus clouds   **B** cirrus and stratus clouds
   C stratus and cumulus clouds **D** cumulus clouds

   (Objective 3)

4 Draw a picture of a scene outside. Stick on pieces of feathers and cotton wool to make clouds.

   Write the name of the clouds and say whether the day will have fair weather or heavy showers.

   (Performance assessment)

5 Look at the sky daily before sunrise and after sunset. Record the time and the date when you see magnificent yellow or red cirrus clouds. Draw the scene and colour it.

   (Performance assessment)

Chapter 2
Air Pollution

Observing

Particles of dirt and poisonous gases **pollute** the air. **Pollutants** are harmful to plants and animals, including humans. People may suffer from bronchitis, asthma and hay fever as a result of air pollution.

In this chapter we will deal with air pollution caused by dirt. Dirt may be dust, smoke or pollen. Dust can be dried mud, sand, fluff or ash. For example, when the Soufrière Hills volcano in Montserrat erupts it pours out tonnes of dust, smoke and ashes into the atmosphere. You may have heard of the Sahara dust coming all the way across the Atlantic ocean from Africa.

Bush fires give off large quantities of smoke and soot into the air. Smokers blow out harmful smoke from their mouths and noses. Cars and factories release fumes into the air and make it dirty.

There is quite a lot of pollen in the air when grasses flower. Many people are sensitive to pollen. They suffer from 'hay fever'.

> **Objectives**
> At the end of the chapter, pupils should be able to:
> - construct a trap for collecting dust particles from the air (page 11).
> - distinguish between the amount of pollution found in different areas, using an air trap (page 12).
> - identify and name two or more air pollutants in a particular area (page 12).

Observing

Activity 1 Making an air trap

Your group will need:
- sticky tape or vaseline
- a styrofoam tray
- glue
- a metal bottle cap
- an old toothbrush (to sweep up dust)
- a sheet of paper (about 10 cm × 11 cm)
- a hand lens

Safety!
- Be careful when using the bottle top as a cutter.

sharp edge

1 Use these materials to make an air trap. The diagram below shows what it should look like.

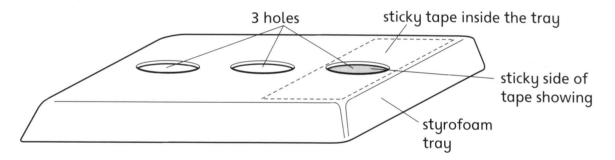

2 Use the bottle top to cut three holes in the bottom of the styrofoam tray.

3 Stick two or three bits of sticky tape across the holes (on the inside of the tray).

4 Turn the tray upside down, so that the sticky side of the tape is on the top.

5 Test your trap by brushing some dust over it. Use the hand lens to observe what collects on your trap.

6 How well did your trap work? Could you make it better?

7 Replace the sticky tape with a clean piece before you use your trap.

8 Your group must make one more trap as homework.

Observing

Activity 2 Using your air trap

Your group will need:
- 4 air traps from Activity 1
- small stones or sticky tape

Safety!
- Be very careful when placing your air traps on walls near the road.

1. Place your air traps in four different places. For example, put one in your school yard (on a box), one on the school wall near the road, one in the yard at home (on a box) and one on your house wall, near the road. Use the stones or sticky tape to keep the traps in place. Label each trap so you know where each one was placed.
2. Collect the traps after one week.
3. Examine each trap with your hand lens.
4. Record your observations in a table like this:

Help each other

Place where trap was	Amount of dirt collected
school wall	a lot

5. Which traps had collected the most dirt particles? Why do you think this was?
6. What type of pollution did you find in the four locations?

Did you know?
- There are hairs in our nostrils. These hairs filter out some of the solid pollutants and prevent them going into our lungs.

Summary
- Pollution is something in a place where it causes harm.
- Air can be polluted by dirt. The dirt can be dust, smoke or pollen.
- These pollutants can cause lung diseases such as bronchitis.

Observing

Test yourself

For each task, write down **A**, **B**, **C** or **D**.

1 X and Y are two air traps.
   Mary says that Trap X can tell the direction the
   pollutants came from. Tom says Trap Y is useless.

   A Only Mary's statement
       is true
   B Only Tom's statement is true
   C Neither Mary's nor Tom's
       statement is true
   D Both Mary's and Tom's
       statements are true

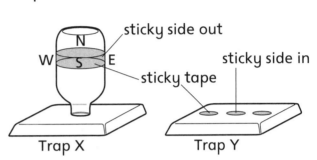

(Objective 2)

2 An air trap was set on a post near a busy dirt road that
   passes through a grass field. Two pollutants that will be
   found on the air trap are

   A cigarette ash and mud   **B** pollen and particles of dry mud
   C fluff and volcanic ash   **D** soot and pollen

(Objective 3)

3 Raj and Susanne each set up an air trap in their school yard.
   Raj's school is in a quiet area and there is no grass in the dirt
   yard. Susanne's school is in a busy area in Port of Spain with
   a concrete yard. Which of the following shows what Raj's
   and Susanne's air traps collected?

	Raj's air trap	Susanne's air trap
A	dry mud	soot
B	pollen	pollen
C	volcanic ash	dry mud
D	rain drops	rain drops

(Objective 2)

13

Chapter 3

Observing

What Growing Plants Need

Plants grow all around you. What do they need to grow?

Activity 1 Let there be light

Your group will need:

- 20 corn or lentil seedlings that have been germinated in a dark box or cupboard
- 2 styrofoam trays (13 cm × 13 cm × 3 cm) filled with garden soil
- an old spoon
- a plastic container full of water
- 2 shoeboxes (31 cm × 15 cm × 8.5 cm) with lids, 1 painted inside with matt black paint or lined with black plastic from a garbage bag
- a ruler

Safety!
- Wash your hands after this activity.

1. Collect 20 corn or lentil seedlings from your teacher. What colour are the seedlings?
2. Plant 10 seedlings in each tray. Label the trays A and B.
3. Measure the height of the seedlings in centimetres.
4. Copy Table 1 in your notebook. Complete the first row.

Table 1

| | Seedlings in tray A (no light) || Seedlings in tray B (in light) ||
	Colour	Height	Colour	Height
When we planted seedlings				
5 days later				

Objectives

At the end of the chapter, pupils should be able to:
- show that growing plants need sunshine (light) (pages 14–15).
- show that growing plants need water (page 16).
- show that growing plants need air (page 17).

Observing

5 Water both sets of seedlings carefully.

6 Place tray A in the shoebox painted black inside. Label the box A. Cover the box.

7 Place tray B in the other shoe box. Label the box B. Do not cover the box.

8 Water both sets of seedlings each day.

9 After five days, remove the cover from box A. Look at the seedlings in both boxes. Discuss what you see.

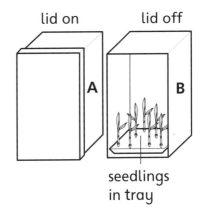

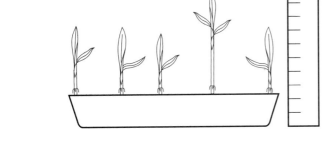

10 Measure the seedlings in both boxes. Now complete Table 1.

11 How are the seedlings in tray A different from those in tray B? Draw one seedling from box A and one from box B.

12 Discuss with your group what happens to plants that do not get enough light. Write a short note about it.

Homework

1 When you go home, look in the kitchen cupboard or refrigerator. Are there any carrots, potatoes or other vegetables that are sprouting? Observe the shoots and leaves carefully.

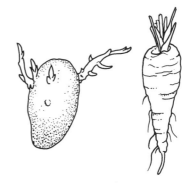

2 If there is a cabbage in the kitchen, look at the outer leaves. Then look at the inner leaves. Is there any difference?

3 Discuss your observations of all the vegetables with your group on the next day.

Observing

Activity 2 Water, water all around

Your group will need:
- 10 germinated seeds, as in Activity 1
- 2 small styrofoam trays filled with garden soil
- an old spoon
- a paper napkin

Safety!
- Wash your hands after the activity.

1. Carefully plant five seedlings in each tray. Label the trays C and D.

2. Place trays C and D side by side in a lighted area.

3. Water tray C moderately (two teaspoons of water) every day for five days. Do not water tray D at all.

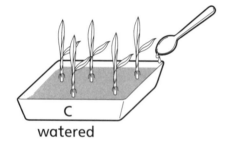
watered

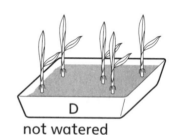
not watered

4. Observe the seedlings every day. Discuss what you see with your group.

5. Make a table like Table 2 in your science book. Write in the table what you see each day.

Table 2

Days	Seedlings in tray C (with water)	Seedlings in tray D (without water)
1		
2		

6. Do plants need water to grow?

Observing

Activity 3 Do plants need air?

Your group will need:
- 2 jam jars
- cotton wool
- 12 dry lentil seeds
- oil
- cool boiled water

1 Put six dry lentil seeds in each jam jar and set up the experiment as shown. Label the jars A and B.

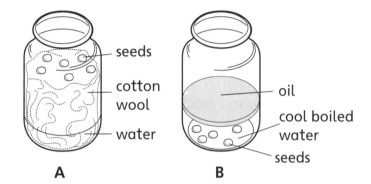

The water in jar B has been boiled and allowed to cool so that there is no air in the water. The layer of oil on the water prevents air from being absorbed into the water. This means that the seeds in jar B have no air.

2 Leave the jars uncovered and place them in a lighted place.

3 Look at your two jars after one week. What do the seeds in jar A look like? What do the seeds in jar B look like?

Everyone in the group must do their part

4 Make a table like Table 3 in your notebook and write down your observations.

Table 3

Seeds in A (with air)	Seeds in B (without air)

5 What happens to seeds that do not get enough air? What do you think would happen to a plant that does not get enough air?

17

Observing

Summary
- Plants need light to grow.
- Plants need water to grow.
- Plants need air to grow.

Test yourself ✏️

For each task, write down **A, B, C** or **D**.

1 James and Anna each had a rose plant in a separate plant pot. Anna watered her plant every day. James was always busy and never watered his plant. Both plants were kept indoors.

   A James's plant grew well and bore lovely roses
   B Anna's plant grew well and bore lovely roses
   C Neither Anna's nor James's plant grew well
   D Both Anna's and James's plants grew well

   (Objective 2)

2 Marsha kept her bean seedling in a closed box, giving it light only from a torch light. Vishnu left his bean seedling out where it could get sunlight.

   A Marsha's plant grew well and Vishnu's plant died
   B Vishnu's plant grew well and Marsha's plant died
   C Neither Vishnu's nor Marsha's plant grew well
   D Both Vishnu's and Marsha's plants grew well

   (Objective 1)

3 In order to grow healthy plants must have

   A good soil, water and light
   B moderate amount of water, light and air
   C water, light and fertiliser
   D a loam soil, a little clay and a little sand

   (Objectives 1, 2 and 3)

Chapter 4 — Observing

Eyes for Seeing

Activity 1 How well can you see?

Your teacher will need a sight chart, like the one in the Teacher's Guide.

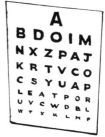

1. When your teacher calls you, go and stand 10 metres from the chart.

2. Read the letters on the chart out loud. Start at the top.

3. When you cannot read the letters clearly, stop.

4. What is the number of the last row of letters that you could read clearly? Write down this number.

5. When all the pupils have read the chart, your teacher will ask: 'Who could read the letters in row 5?'

6. If you could read the letters in row 5, your eyesight is good. If you could read the rows after row 5, your eyesight is very good. If you could not read as far as row 5, your eyesight is poor.

People who cannot see clearly things that are far away are **short-sighted**.

People who can see things far away but cannot see things that are near very clearly are **long-sighted**.

Objectives

At the end of the chapter, pupils should be able to:
- identify pupils in the class with poor and/or good eyesight (pages 19–20).
- describe changes in the appearance of their eyes in response to dim light and bright light or to approaching objects (pages 20–22).
- identify ways of keeping the eyes clean and healthy (page 23).

19

Observing

Activity 2 Are you short-sighted or long-sighted?

1 Pick up this book. Hold it so that you can read it easily.

2 Are you holding the book very close to your eyes?
If you are, you are short-sighted.

3 Are you holding the book as far away from your eyes as you can?
Then you are long-sighted.

Most people need to hold a book about 25 centimetres from their eyes.

The **pupil** is a hole at the front of your eye. You see an object when light from the object enters your eye through the pupil.

The **iris** is the coloured ring round the pupil.

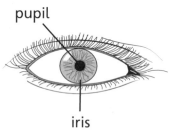

Diagram 1

Activity 3 Eyes and the dark

Your group will need:

- a watch with a second hand

Work with another child in your group.

Respect others

1 Look at the eyes of your partner. Look for the iris and the pupil (see diagram 1).

2 Copy diagram 2 in your book. Draw what the iris and pupil of your partner look like.

Diagram 2

Observing

3 Ask your partner to close one eye for 30 seconds. After 30 seconds say, 'Open!'

4 Look again at the iris and pupil of the eye that was closed. Draw what the iris and pupil look like now.

5 Let your partner look at your eye and do steps 2, 3 and 4.

6 How did the pupil of your eye change after you closed it for 30 seconds?

Activity 4 Eyes and the light

Your group will need:

- a torch light

Work with a partner.

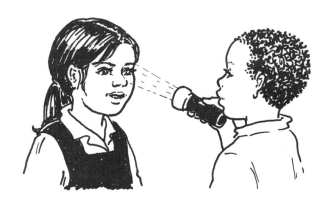

1 Shine the torch light into one of your partner's eyes. What happens to the iris and the pupil? Exchange roles.

2 Draw the iris and the pupil as you saw them, in your notebook.

3 How did the pupil of the eye change when you shone a light into the eye?

If there is not much light, the pupils of your eyes open wider. This lets more light get into your eye, so you can see better.

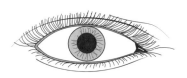

If there is a lot of light, it might damage your eyes. So the pupils get smaller. They let less light into the eyes.

Observing

Activity 5 Eyes and moving things

Your group will need:

- a clean handkerchief

Work with a partner.

Behave responsibly

1 Look at each other's eyes.

2 When your teacher says, 'start', count the number of times your partner blinks.
   Your partner will count how many times you blink.

3 Your teacher will say, 'stop' after three minutes.

4 Make a table like this:

Name	Number of blinks in 3 minutes

5 Who blinked most in your group?

6 Who blinked least in your group?

7 Suddenly, but carefully, wave a handkerchief in front of your partner's eyes.
   Did your partner blink? Why?

Observing

Most people blink five, six or seven times every minute.

When you blink, tears spread over your eyeballs and keep them moist.

Tears wash away dust from your eyes. They also kill germs that enter your eyes.

Speak quietly

When an object suddenly approaches your eyes you blink. This helps to protect the eyes from damage.

Look after your eyes

Here are some rules to help you look after your eyesight.

- Do not look at the sun.
- Never clean your eyes with a towel used by other people.

- Use eye goggles when you work with materials that may fly up into your eyes.
- If you need to go up near to the board in class to read it, ask your parents to have your eyes tested.

- Do not watch television for too long at a time.
- Do not watch television in a dark or very bright room.
- Make sure the television has a clear picture.

- If you get a blow on the eye, go to bed and put an ice-bag on the eye. Your parents may need to take you to the doctor.
- When something gets in your eye, wash it out with lots of cool, previously boiled water. If it still hurts, let your parents take you to the doctor. Do not rub the eye.

Observing

Summary

- Some people cannot see things that are far away clearly. They are short-sighted.
- Some people cannot see things that are near clearly but can see things that are far away. They are long-sighted.
- The pupil is a small hole that lets light into the eye.
- In dim light the pupil gets bigger.
- In bright light the pupil gets smaller.
- If an object approaches your eyes suddenly you blink.
- Blinking protects your eyes. It also keeps the eyes moist.
- You must look after your eyes.

Test yourself

For each task, write down **A**, **B**, **C** or **D**.

1 Mohun got up one night and looked into the mirror – only the dim night light was on. In the morning he looked at his eyes again, this time using a bright torch. Mohun saw

   A large pupils in dim light and small pupils in bright light
   B small pupils in dim light and large pupils in bright light
   C small pupils in dim light and small pupils in bright light
   D large pupils in dim light and large pupils in bright light

   Give a reason for your choice.

   (Objective 2)

2 Your eyes are protected from dust and germs by

   A tears in your eyes   B washing them at least 10 times a day
   C blowing out the dust   D wearing glasses

   (Objective 3)

Chapter 5 — Measuring

Thermometers

How do you tell if something is hot or cold? You can tell if something is warmer or colder than you are by touching it. But that is not very accurate.

We use a **thermometer** to measure how hot or cold something is.

Activity 1 Is it hot? Is it cold?

Your group will need:
- a teacher-made thermometer
- crayons (red, yellow, green, blue)
- ice cubes in a cup
- hot water (on your teacher's desk) not more than 50°C

— Safety! —
- Be very careful when you place your thermometer in the hot water. Do this only when your teacher is there with you.

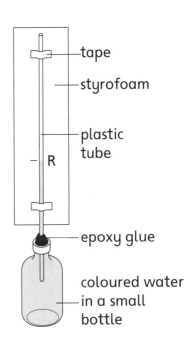

1. Hold the thermometer by the styrofoam, not the bottle. Is the red liquid moving?
2. Put a green mark at the level of the liquid in the tube. Mark R for **room temperature**. This shows how hot or cold the room is.

Objectives
At the end of the chapter pupils should be able to:
- read and state thermometer readings on a Celsius thermometer (page 27).
- measure and state the boiling and freezing points of water in degrees Celsius (pages 27–28).
- measure and state the body temperature in degrees Celsius (pages 27–28).

25

Measuring

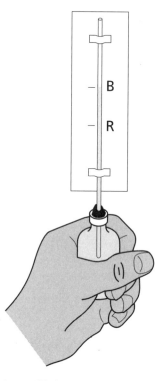

3 Hold the bottle in your hand. Watch the red liquid. When it stops moving put a yellow line at the level of the liquid.

4 Write B next to the yellow line. This shows your **body temperature**. It shows how hot your body is.

5 Go up to your teacher's desk. Put the bottle into the hot water. What happens?

6 When the liquid stops moving, draw a red line and mark it H for hot.

7 Discuss with your group what you think will happen when you put the bottle of your thermometer in the glass with the ice and water.

8 Put the bottle in the glass and watch what happens.

9 When the red liquid stops moving, mark a blue line. Label it M for melting.

The thermometer you used in Activity 1 now has a **scale**. The scale shows four temperatures: ice melting, room temperature, your body temperature, and hot.

A real thermometer can measure lots of different temperatures. The scale on a real thermometer measures temperature in **degrees Celsius**. If the liquid in the thermometer is at the mark labelled 12, it means that the temperature of the bulb of the thermometer is 12 degrees Celsius (12°C for short).

26

Measuring

Activity 2 What temperature does each of the thermometers here show?

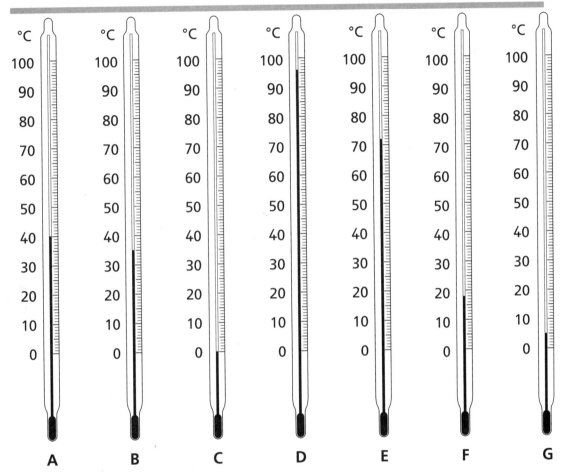

A   B   C   D   E   F   G

The boiling point of pure water is 100 °C.
This means that water boils at 100 °C.

The freezing point of pure water is 0 °C.
This means that water freezes at 0 °C.

The melting point of pure ice is 0 °C.
This means that ice melts at 0 °C.

Normal body temperature is 37 °C.
A person with body temperature 38 °C
to 40 °C has a fever.

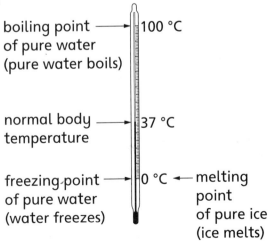

Room temperature in Trinidad and
Tobago is usually between 30 °C and 33 °C during the day.

Measuring

If your teacher has some real thermometers you can try this activity.

Activity 3 How hot is it in degrees Celsius?

Your group will need:
- an alcohol thermometer
- 3 ice cubes and some water in a plastic container

1. Look carefully at the thermometer. Discuss the markings on it. Everyone in your group must be able to read the numbers. What do the spaces between the numbers stand for?

2. Put the bulb of the thermometer in the ice and water. Wait until the liquid in the thermometer stops moving.

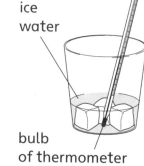

3. Read the temperature on the scale. When everyone in your group has looked at the scale and agreed on the temperature, write it in your book.

4. Hold the bulb of the thermometer in your hand. When the liquid stops going up, read the temperature. This is your body temperature. Let everyone measure their body temperature. Did you all have the same body temperature?

Summary
- We use a thermometer to measure how hot or cold something is (its temperature).
- A thermometer measures temperature in degrees Celsius (°C).
- Pure water boils at 100°C.
- Pure water freezes at 0°C. Pure ice melts at 0°C.
- Normal body temperature is 37°C.
- If a person's body temperature is between 38°C and 40°C we say that person has a fever.
- Room temperature is the temperature of the air in a room. In Trinidad and Tobago it is usually between 30°C and 33°C during the day.

Measuring

Test yourself

For each task, write down **A**, **B**, **C** or **D**.

Tasks 1 to 4 are based on the drawings below.
The thermometers A, B, C and D are graduated the same as thermometer X.

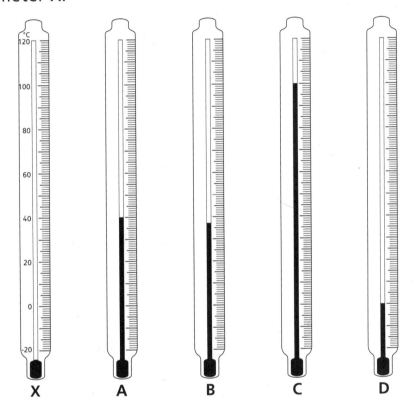

1. The thermometer showing the boiling point of pure water.

   (Objectives 1 and 2)

2. The thermometer showing normal body temperature.

   (Objectives 1 and 3)

3. The thermometer showing the freezing point of pure water.

   (Objectives 1 and 2)

4. The thermometer showing Anna's temperature when she has a fever.

   Give a reason for your choice. **(Objectives 1 and 3)**

29

Chapter 6　　　　　　　　　　　　　　Measuring

Making a Balance

Activity 1　Arranging masses

Your group will need:

- a pump-top plastic bottle $\frac{3}{4}$ filled with sand
- a wooden block
- a styrofoam block
- a tennis ball
- a ping-pong ball

1 Arrange the items in order, from the lightest to the heaviest. Show your teacher. How did you decide how light or heavy an item was?

You can compare how heavy different objects are by lifting them. We say that a heavy object has more **mass** than a light one.

To compare masses more accurately you need to use a **balance**.

Activity 2　Making an equal arm balance

Your group will need:

- an empty plastic bottle with a pump handle
- a ruler
- a bulldog clip
- a nail
- 2 styrofoam cups or trays
- sand
- string
- a picture of an equal arm balance

Safety!

- Be careful when using tools. If you have never used a particular tool before, ask your teacher for help.
- Handle nails carefully.

Objectives

At the end of the chapter pupils should be able to:
- construct an equal arm balance (pages 30–31).
- measure different masses using the balance (pages 31–33).

Measuring

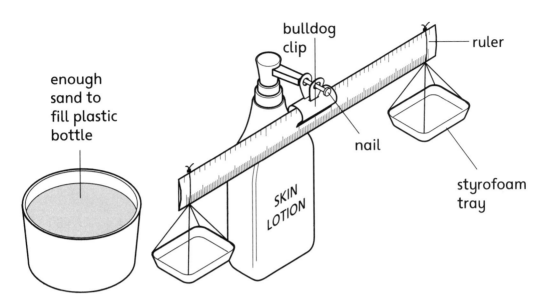

1. Discuss the balance in the picture with your group.
2. Fill the plastic bottle with sand.
3. Put the nail through the bulldog clip. Fix it into the bottle top as shown in the diagram.
4. Put the ruler in the clip. Make sure the ruler is level.
5. Make holes in the styrofoam trays or cups. Tie string to them so that you can hang them from each end of the ruler. Make sure the ruler is still level.
6. Make any changes to improve your balance if you need to.

Activity 3   Using your balance

Your group will need:
- your equal arm balance
- 4 black film cans (one empty, two with equal amounts of sand in them, one with more sand)

1. Put the empty can in one tray of your balance. Put one of the other cans in the other tray. What happens?
2. Take the empty can off the balance. Put one of the other cans in its place.
   What happens now?

Measuring

3 Can you use your balance to find which two cans have the same mass?
Discuss your ideas in your group and then try it.

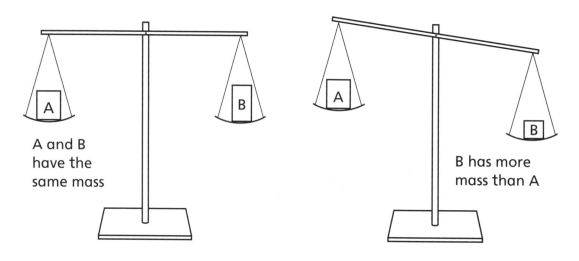

A and B have the same mass

B has more mass than A

If the objects in the two trays (or pans) of an equal arm balance have the same mass, the balance will be level.

If one object is heavier than the other, that side of the balance will go down.

Activity 4 Comparing masses

Your group will need:

- a washer, a bolt, a screw, a soft drink bottle cap, a small wooden block (or other small objects)
- twenty 5¢ coins

1 Put the washer in one of the pans of the balance.

2 Add 5¢ coins to the other pan until the balance is level again.

3 How many coins did you need? The mass of the washer is equal to the mass of this number of coins.

Measuring

4 Do this with all the objects. Copy and complete this table:

Object	Number of coins to balance object
washer	

Summary
- An equal arm balance is used to compare the masses of objects.
- When the balance arm is level, the objects in the two pans have the same mass.

Test yourself

For each task, write down **A**, **B**, **C** or **D**.

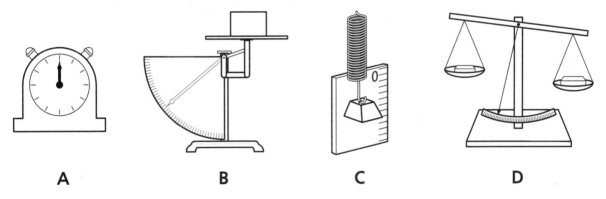

A   B   C   D

1 Which of the above diagrams is an equal arm balance?

(Objective 1)

2
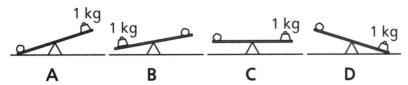

A   B   C   D

The object with mass that is greater than 1 kg is at

A   B   C   D

Give a reason for your choice.

(Objective 2)

Chapter 7

Measuring Forces with Springs

A **force** is a push or a pull. Forces act on things.

Activity 1   Balancing forces

Work with a partner.

You will need:
- a box or other solid object

Take turns answering questions

1   Push the box across the table.

2   Let your partner push it back again.

3   Now both push at the same time. Try to push just as hard as each other, so that the box does not move.

In Activity 1 there were two forces (pushes) acting on the box. But it did not move. The two forces were the same, but they were in opposite directions. The forces were **balanced**.

Objectives

At the end of the chapter pupils should be able to:
- state a rule, that if an object does not move, the forces acting upon it must be in balance (page 34).
- state a rule, that attaching a weight to a spring increases the force pulling on the spring so that it stretches (pages 35–36).
- demonstrate with a spring balance whether two objects have the same or different weights (page 37).

Measuring

Activity 2 How the earth pulls

Your group will need:
- 2 opaque 1 litre plastic bottles, one with more sand in it than the other
- a ball of plasticine

1 Lift the bottle as in the picture.
   Do you feel the bottle pulling from your hand?

2 Let the bottle go. What happens?

3 Throw the plasticine up to just over your head.

4 Did the plasticine go up, up and away? Or did it fall to earth?

5 Jump as high as you can. Did you go up, up and away?

6 Lift both bottles.
   Does the earth pull on both bottles with the same force?
   How do you know?

The earth pulls things towards itself. That is why things fall to earth.

A pull is a force. The earth-pull is a force.

The earth-pull (force) on an object is called its **weight**.
Weight is a force. The direction of this force is down.

35

Measuring

Activity 3 How forces affect a spring

Your group will need:
- a light spring or rubber band
- 2 black film cans, one filled with sand
- 2 hooks
- sticky tape

Safety!
- The end of the spring may scratch you if you are not careful.

1. Examine the spring with your group.
2. Discuss with your group what you can do with the spring.
3. Pull it a little. What happens?
4. Pull it harder. What happens now?
5. Copy and complete this sentence in your book:
   The harder you pull the spring the _____.

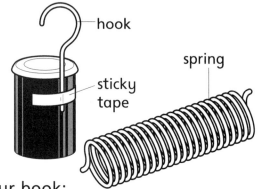

Your teacher will put two black film cans on your desk. Do not touch them.

6. How are the two cans alike?
7. Pick up the cans, one in each hand. How are the two cans different?
8. Hook one can onto the spring.
   How far does the spring stretch?
9. Now try it with the other can.
10. Which can stretches the spring more?

Respect yourself

If you hang an object on the end of a spring, the weight of the object makes the spring stretch. An object with a large weight will make the spring stretch more.

Measuring

Activity 4 Which has more weight?

Your group will need:
- a spring balance (low cost)
- the 2 black film cans used in Activity 3

Safety!
- Handle the hook on the spring balance with care.

1 Label the two cans A and B.

2 Hold the hook of the spring balance and pull it down.

3 Copy and complete this sentence in your book:

   The more force I use to pull on the spring balance, the _____ the spring _____.

4 Can you use the spring balance to find which film can is heavier? Discuss this with your group.

5 Put can A on the hook of the spring balance. Observe what happens.

6 Take off can A and put can B on the hook of the spring balance.

7 Discuss what you observe with your group. Which film can do you think is heavier than the other?

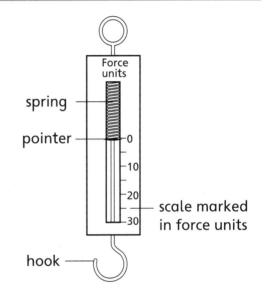

Summary
- Weight is a force.
- The weight of an object is a measure of the earth's pull on the object.
- The direction of the force (called weight) is down.
- A spring stretches when a force (a pull) acts on it.
- An object with a large weight stretches a spring more than an object with a small weight.

Measuring

Test yourself

1 Copy and complete the passage below.

A spring _____ when a pulling force is put on it. The bigger the force, the _____ it stretches. For this reason a spring can be used as a _____ measurer.

(Objective 2)

2 Copy and complete the statement below.

If the forces acting on an object are in balance the object does _____ .

(Objective 1)

For task 3, write down **A**, **B**, **C** or **D**.

3 The spring balances below are graduated in force units. Two objects that weigh the same in the diagrams are

A 1 and 2   B 3 and 4
C 2 and 3   D 1 and 4

(Objective 3)

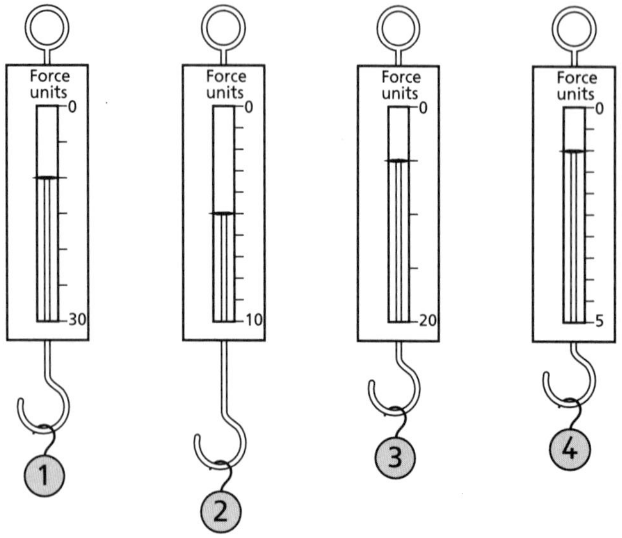

38

Chapter 8

Classifying

Separating Materials from Mixtures

In a **mixture** there are two or more substances together. You can separate the **components** of a mixture.

Activity 1 The mixture

Your group will need:

- a clear plastic container with a lid
- a styrofoam tray
- a film can filled with gravel
- a film can filled with coarse sand
- a film can filled with fine sand
- a sheet of newspaper

1 Empty the three film cans onto the newspaper in three separate heaps. Look at each heap carefully.

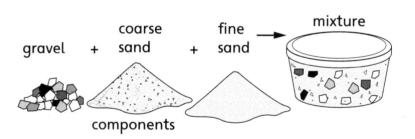

Safety!
- Wash your hands after the activity.

2 Tip all three heaps into the plastic container.

3 Put the lid on the container. Shake it hard.

4 Discuss with your group what you see in the container now. Write down the items you can see.

5 Do you think you could separate the gravel, the coarse sand and the fine sand?

Objectives

At the end of the chapter pupils should be able to:
- demonstrate a method of separating the components of a mixture (pages 40–41).
- order the parts of the mixture according to size (pages 40–41).
- demonstrate that the amount of each component in a mixture can be found by comparing the weights of the components (pages 41–42).

Classifying

Activity 2 Separating a mixture

Your group will need:

- marbles or beads of three different sizes (20 of each), mixed together in a container
- 3 styrofoam cups
- a watch with a second hand or a digital watch

Listen to other people's ideas

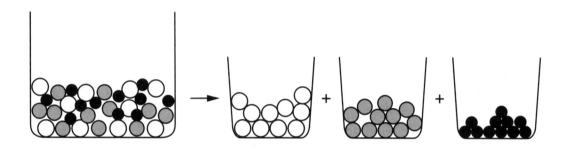

1 Collect the mixture of beads from your teacher.

2 Discuss with your group how you can separate the components of the mixture. When you all agree, make one member of the group the time keeper and give him or her the watch.

3 When the time keeper says, 'start', begin to separate the mixture into its components.

4 How long did it take you to do it?

5 Order the components of your mixture from largest to smallest.

You could separate a mixture of sand and gravel in the same way you separated beads or marbles in Activity 2. But it would be very difficult!

Classifying

Activity 3 Using sieves

Your group will need:
- the mixture of gravel, coarse sand and fine sand from Activity 1
- 2 sieves each with a different size mesh
- 1 styrofoam tray
- newspaper
- equal arm balance (made in Chapter 6)
- thirty 1¢ coins
- spring balance (low cost) or force meter

Safety!
- Wash your hands after the activity.

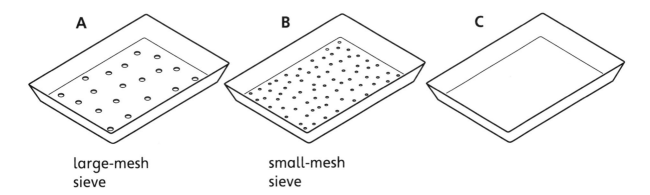

large-mesh sieve   small-mesh sieve

1 How could you use the apparatus you have to separate the mixture into its components? Discuss this in your group.

2 Put all the mixture in sieve A. Shake the sieve over the newspaper. What do you observe?

3 What is left in sieve A?

4 Tip the mixture on the newspaper into sieve B. Shake it over the newspaper.

5 What is left in sieve B?

6 Put what fell through sieve B into the styrofoam tray. Label it C.

7 Use the spring balance to find the weight of the material in sieve A.

Respect each other

Classifying

8 Do the same with the components in B and C. Make a table like this to show your results:

Component	Weight (in force units)
A: gravel	
B: coarse sand	
C: fine sand	

Summary
- A mixture is made up of two or more components.
- The components of a mixture can be seen and can be separated physically.

Test yourself

For this task, write down **A, B, C** or **D**.

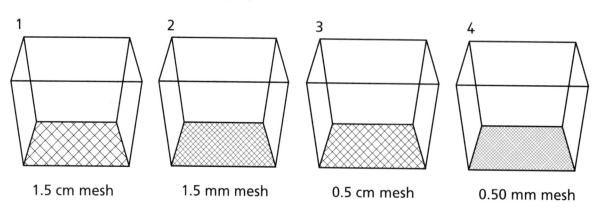

1   1.5 cm mesh   2   1.5 mm mesh   3   0.5 cm mesh   4   0.50 mm mesh

1 To separate a mixture of coarse sand, dry clay, fine sand and pebbles John should arrange the four sieves shown above from top to bottom in the following order.

A 1 2 3 4   B 1 3 2 4   C 4 2 3 1   D 3 4 2 1

Give a reason for your choice.

(Objective 1)

42

Chapter 9

Classifying

Floating and Sinking

Activity 1 Will it float?

Your group will need:

- an onion, a potato, a tomato, an eraser, a lime, a small piece of wood, a pencil, a piece of styrofoam, a stone, a metal paperclip, a candle, a washer, a sponge, a red bean seed, a crayon
- a small clear plastic container
- about a teaspoonful of cooking oil
- a large ice-cream tub $\frac{3}{4}$ full of water

Safety!
- Do not put the objects into your mouth.

1. Discuss with your group whether the objects you have will float in water. When you all agree, copy Table 1 and complete columns 1 and 2.

2. Pour the cooking oil into the small container of water. Observe. Complete column 3 of your table.

3. Put the other things one at a time into the tub of water. Observe. Complete column 3.

Table 1

Object	Do you think it will float?	Did it float?

Objectives

At the end of this chapter pupils should be able to:
- demonstrate a method of separating objects that float and those that do not float (page 43).
- identify and demonstrate a method for making objects float which normally do not float (page 44).
- demonstrate and state that the type of material is important in determining whether an object will sink or float (pages 45–46).
- demonstrate and state that the shape of an object is important in determining whether an object will sink or float (pages 46–47).

Classifying

Activity 2   How can you make it float?

Your group will need:

- an ice-cream tub full of water
- a coin
- a flat piece of wood
- 2 clear plastic containers
- 2 tablespoons of salt
- a raw egg, a piece of carrot, 6 peanuts (3 with skins and 3 without), a piece of potato, lime or orange seeds

Safety!
- Handle the egg carefully.
- Do not put the objects in your mouth.

1. Put the coin in the tub of water. Does it float?
2. Put the wood in the water. Does it float?
3. Discuss with your group how you could make the coin float. Try it.
4. Fill one of the other containers with water to about 3 cm from the top.
5. Place the egg, potato, carrot, nuts and seeds, one at a time, in the water. Write a sentence to say what you observe.
6. Fill the other container with water. Add the salt. Stir until the salt dissolves.
7. Place the egg, potato, carrot, nuts and seeds in the salt water. Write down what you observe.

You can make things float by putting them on something that *does* float. A raft or a boat can carry heavy objects that would sink if you put them in the water. Some things that do not float in fresh water will float in salt water.

Did you know?

- The world's saltiest water is in the Dead Sea in Israel. Even if you do not swim you will not sink in the Dead Sea. You can even read a book quite comfortably.

Classifying

Project

Observe the water-line on the boat in the diagram. The boat is in a large fresh-water river that takes cargo to and from larger boats at sea.

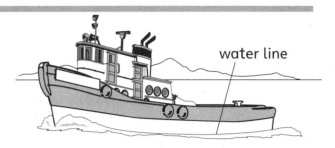

boat in fresh-water river

1. Discuss with your group where the water-line on the boat may be when the boat goes out to sea. When you all agree, draw the boat and put the sea-water water-line on the boat. Say why you drew the line where you did.

2. Find out about the Plimsoll line on ships. Why is the Plimsoll line important?

Activity 3 Does it matter what it is made of?

Your group will need:
- a 1¢ coin, a small piece of wood, a marble, a cork, a stone, a pencil, a large nail, a small candle, a stick, or other similar small objects
- a large ice-cream tub full of water

Safety!
- Do not put any of the objects in your mouth.

1. Place the items, one at a time, in the water.
2. Discuss with your group what each object is made of.
3. Copy and complete Table 2 in your notebook.

Table 2

Object	What is it made of?	Did it float?

45

Classifying

4 Make a list of materials that floated.
  Make another list of materials that sank.

Whether an object sinks or floats depends on what it is made of.

Things made of wood or plastic usually float.

Things made of metal, glass or stone usually sink.

Activity 4 Does the shape make a difference?

Your group will need:
- 25 1¢ coins or similar coins
- 2 pieces of aluminium foil 10 cm × 10 cm
- an ice-cream tub full of water

1 Wrap the coins in one sheet of foil.

2 Place the wrapped coins in the tub of water.

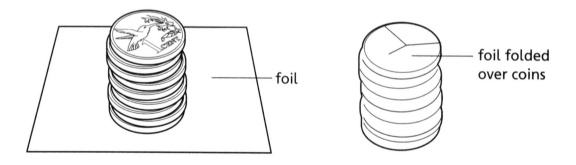

3 Write down what you observe.

4 Discuss with your group how you can shape the other piece of foil so that it will float with the coins in it. When you all agree, draw a picture of your foil 'boat'.

5 Make your boat. Put it in the tub of water. Does it float?

6 Place the coins in it gently, one by one. How many coins will it carry without sinking?

Speak quietly

The foil boat in Activity 4 floats because it is hollow and

Classifying

contains much air. A steel ship will float for the same reason. Boats have even been made of concrete! But they still float, because they are hollow.

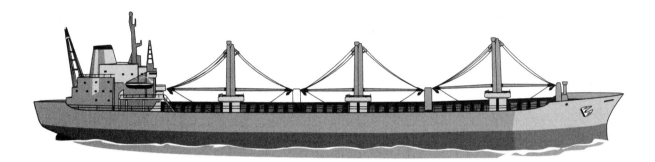

Summary
- Some objects float and some sink in tap water.
- An object that previously sank may float if you put it on top of something else that floats.
- Some objects that do not float in tap water will float in salt water.
- Whether an object will sink or float depends on what it is made of.
- An object made of a material that normally sinks will float if it is shaped so that it can hold much air.

Test yourself

For each task, write down **A**, **B**, **C** or **D**.

1 Vashti and John wanted to separate ten objects into those that float and those that do not float. Vashti, who lives near the sea, filled a bucket with sea water and put the objects in. John filled a bucket with tap water and put the objects in. Whose method is correct?

   A Only Vashti's method is correct
   B Only John's method is correct
   C Both John's and Vashti's methods are correct
   D Neither Vashti's nor John's method is correct

(Objective 1)

Classifying

2 Sherida put a marble in a deflated balloon and put it into a bucket of water. The marble and balloon sank to the bottom. Sherida could make the marble in the balloon float by

   A squeezing out the air from the balloon
   B flattening the balloon and placing it gently on the water surface
   C placing the marble as near as possible to the mouth of the balloon
   D blowing up the balloon

   (Objective 2)

3 A piece of wood with a mass of 50 g and a stone with a mass of 5 g were placed in a bucket of water. The wood floated and the stone sank because floating and sinking depend on

   A the size of the object
   B the type of material
   C the volume of water
   D the mass of the object

   (Objective 3)

4 Yasmin put a block of aluminium into a bucket of water. The block sank. A blacksmith friend hammered the aluminium block into the shape of a flat bottom boat. To Yasmin's surprise the piece of aluminium floated. The aluminium floated because

   A boats can float
   B there was a large amount of air space
   C boats made of iron and steel float so one of aluminium will float
   D there was not enough water in the bucket

   (Objective 4)

Chapter 10
An Aquarium

Classifying

Here is a set of things in an aquarium.

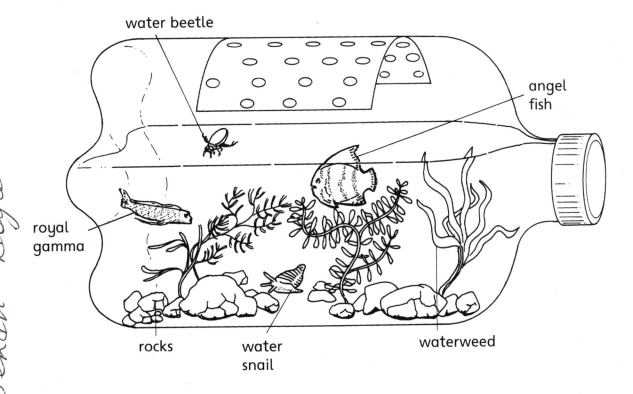

Activity 1 Classifying things in an aquarium

Your group will need:

- the school aquarium, if the school has one OR a low-cost one (see Book 7 of this series) OR the picture above

1 Look carefully at all the things in the aquarium. Can you name them all?

Objective

At the end of the chapter pupils should be able to:
- group organisms found in an aquarium into sets and subsets (pages 49–50).

49

Classifying

2 Make a large diagram like this one in your notebook and complete it.

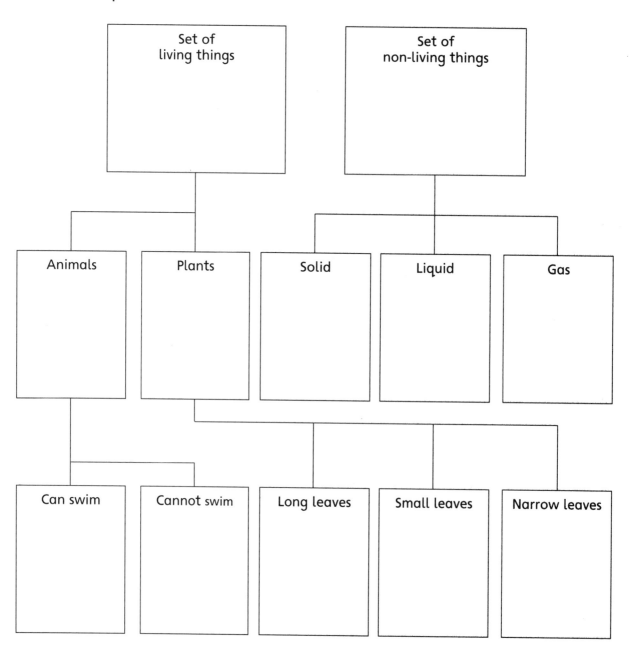

> **Summary**
> - The things in an aquarium can be divided into two sets: living things and non-living things.
> - The sets of things can be divided into subsets.

50

Classifying

Test yourself

For this task, write down **A, B, C** or **D**.

1 We may group things found in our class aquarium into which of the following?

A

```
        living                    non-living
       /      \                   /        \
   animals   plants          gravel     plastic
    /  \       |
  fins  no   float
        fins   |
              sink
```

B

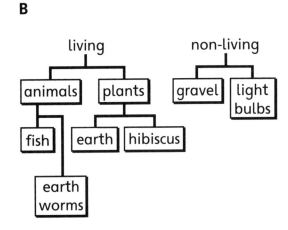

C

```
        living                    non-living
       /      \                   /        \
   plants   animals          stones     clay
    / \      /    \
  rose bean shark salmon
```

D

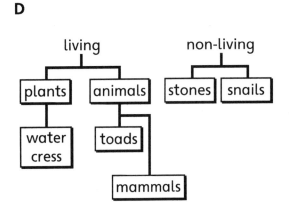

(Objective 1)

51

Chapter 11 Classifying
Seeds and Leaves

Seeds

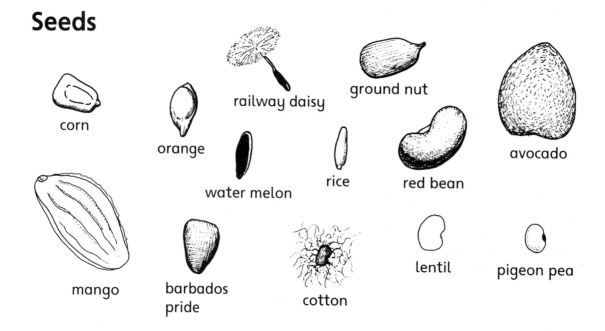

Activity 1 Looking at seeds

Your group will need:

- as many different kinds of seed as possible (the picture shows some that you might use)

Safety!

- Do not put any of the seeds into your mouth.

1 Make a table like Table 1 in your notebook:

Table 1 *Seeds*

Name of seed	Size	Shape	Colour	Texture
lentil	small	round and flat	brown	smooth

Objectives

At the end of the chapter pupils should be able to:
- classify seeds according to size, shape, colour and texture (pages 52–53).
- classify leaves according to shape, colour, edges, texture (page 54).

Classifying

2. Look at each of your seeds in turn. Is it big, medium size or small? Write your answer in the 'Size' column of Table 1.

3. What shape is the seed? Describe it in the table.

4. What colour is the seed? Write it in your table.

5. Is the seed hard or soft? Does it feel smooth or rough? Is it hairy or waxy? Does it have little hooks or a feathery parachute? Write the answers to these questions in the 'Texture' column of your table.

6. Group all the large seeds together, all the medium-sized seeds together, and all the small seeds together. Show your teacher.

Leaves

Bring materials to school when asked

Leaves can be different shapes. Some are **simple leaves**:

Compound leaves are made up of several smaller leaflets:

Leaves can have smooth edges or jagged edges:

53

Classifying

Activity 2 Looking at leaves

Your group will need:

- as many different kinds of leaves as you can find (the picture shows some examples)

Safety!
- Do not put leaves into your mouth. Wash your hands after this activity.

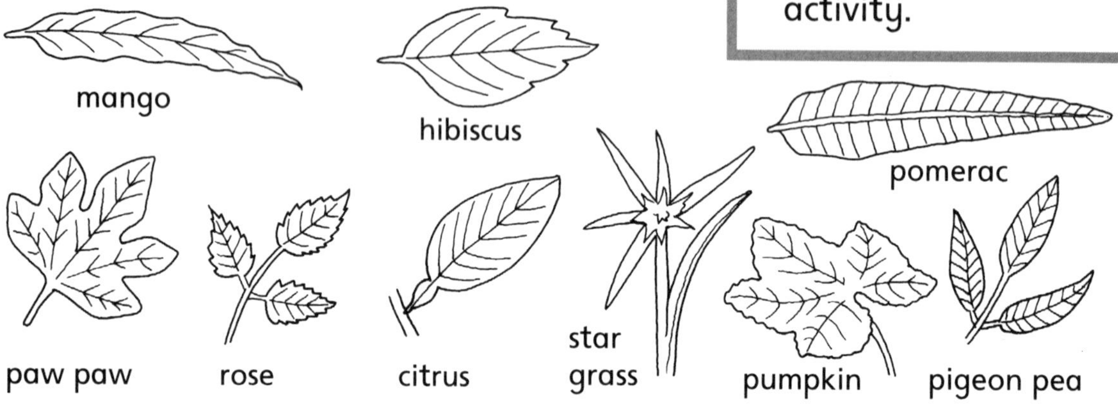

mango, hibiscus, pomerac, paw paw, rose, citrus, star grass, pumpkin, pigeon pea

1 Make a table like Table 2 in your notebook.

Table 2 *Leaves*

Name of leaf	Shape	Colour	Edges	Texture

2 Look at each of your leaves in turn. Write its name in the table.
What shape is it? Is it long and thin, or short and wide? Is it a simple leaf or a compound leaf? Describe it in the 'Shape' column of Table 2.

3 What colour is your leaf? Write it down in your table.

4 Does it have smooth edges, or jagged edges?

5 What kind of texture does the leaf have? Is it smooth and glossy, or rough and hairy? When you all agree, write it in the last column of the table.

Classifying

> **Summary**
> - Seeds are of different sizes, shapes, colours and textures.
> - Leaves are of different sizes, shapes, colour and textures.
> - Leaves may be simple or compound.
> - Some leaves have smooth edges, others have jagged edges.

Test yourself

For each task, write down **A, B, C** or **D**.

	Seeds	Colour of seed				Size of seed	
		black	brown	white	yellow	larger than 6 cm	smaller than 2 cm
A	mango				✔	✔	
B	coconut		✔			✔	
C	black eye	✔					✔
D	corn		✔				✔

1. A student put ticks (✔) in the columns to show the colour and size of the seeds listed in the table above. However, the only seed that is correctly described is at

    A   B   C   D

    (Objective 1)

2.

    Leaves that are compound and jagged are shown at

    A 1 and 2   **B** 1 and 4   **C** 2 and 6   **D** 1 and 5

    (Objective 2)

Chapter 12 — Classifying

A Trip to the Beach

On the beach you can find lots of plants and animals.

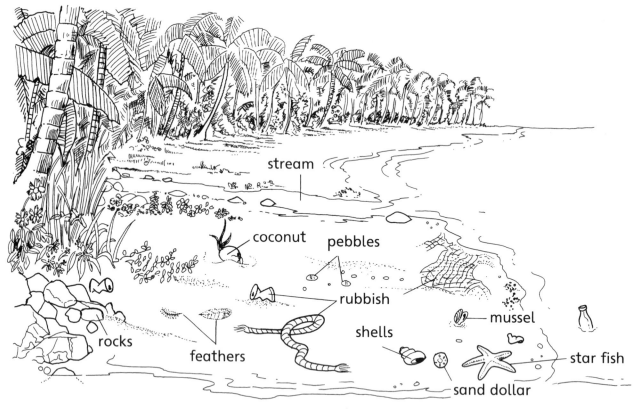

In the sea, there are also lots of plants and animals.

Objectives

At the end of the chapter pupils should be able to:
- identify and state how some animals and plants found at the seaside are alike or different (pages 57–58).
- classify animals collected at the seaside according to physical characteristics or how they behave (pages 59–60).

Classifying

Activity 1 A field trip to a beach

Your group will need:
- plastic bottles, boxes and bags with twist ties
- a hand lens
- a metric tape measure

> **Safety!**
> - Do not go into the sea.
> - Stay with your group always.
> - Wear gloves or loosely tied plastic bags on your hands when you pick things up.
> - Watch out for broken glass.

1. Your teacher will tell you which part of the beach your group is going to look at. Use the tape measure to measure it. Draw a rough sketch map of the area, like this:

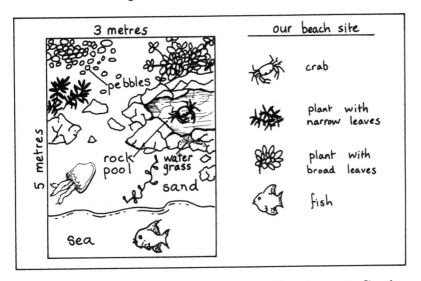

2. Mark on your sketch map any plants you find growing.
   What sort of plants grow close to the water?
   What sort of plants grow further away from the water?
   If there is a stream running down your part of the beach, what sort of plants grow near it?

3. Pick up any animals you find on your beach site. If they are alive, put them in bottles or boxes with some sea water. Do not touch a jellyfish – it stings!
   You might find dead animals too.

Classifying

4 Look carefully at the animals you have found. Use the hand lens. Are any of the animals like each other? How are they different from each other?
   Are the animals you found near the water different from the animals you found away from the water?

5 Collect some other things you find on the beach. You may find shells, stones, seaweed, litter such as bottles and plastic food wrappers, feathers and so on.

6 Your teacher may want you to take the animals you have collected back to school. If not, make drawings of them. Then put the animals and plants you collected back where you found them. Put the litter in the nearest litter bin.

Activity 2 Seaside plants

Here are some plants that grow at the seaside:

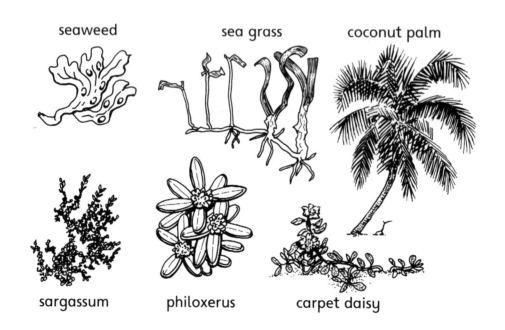

1 Look at the picture carefully.
2 In what ways are the plants like each other?
3 In what ways are the different plants unlike each other?

58

Classifying

Activity 3 Seaside animals

Here are some animals that you might find at the seaside:

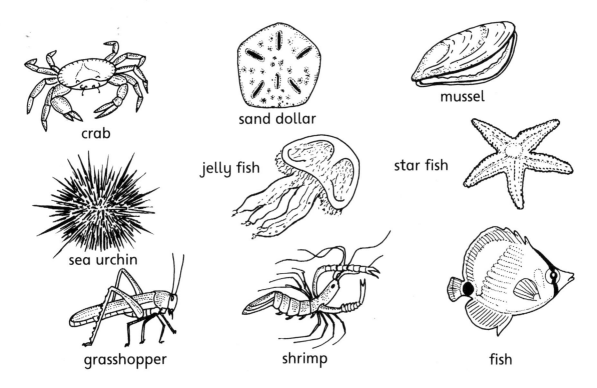

1. Discuss with your group which animals you think are like each other in some way. Divide the animals into two or three groups. For example, all the animals that swim in the sea might be one group, and all the animals that live on the beach another.

Animals that live in the water	Animals that live on the beach

2. Divide each of your groups into smaller groups. For example, animals that have legs and animals that do not have legs.
3. Can you think of other ways that the animals differ? Discuss this.

Classifying

4 Make a diagram like this and write in the names of the animals in the picture on page 59 in the correct boxes. You could add some more subsets to your diagram.

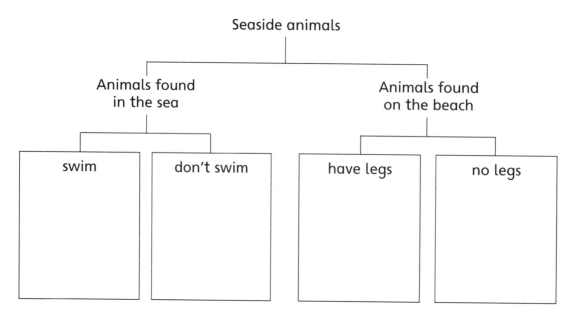

5 If you brought back animals from the seaside in Activity 1, try to add them to your diagram. If you do not know their names, draw pictures of them.

Marine debris

Marine debris is rubbish that people throw into the sea. You might find fishing lines, nets, rope, plastic bags, metal ring pulls from cans and so on. These can wrap around sea animals and even strangle them.

Fish and other animals may swallow plastic bags (they look like jellyfish). This can cause them to suffocate or to starve to death.

Marine debris affects people too. It is ugly and keeps tourists away. Cleaning it up costs money. Fishing line, nets and plastic bags entangle boat propellors. Sharp pieces of glass on the beach may injure bathers.

Classifying

We can prevent marine debris in these ways:

(1) put all trash in trash cans

(2) make less trash, by recycling and re-using waste

(3) spread the word about the harmful effects of marine debris.

> **Summary**
> - The plants and animals found at the seaside are alike in some ways and different in others.
> - You can classify seaside animals into different groups.
> - We must try to reduce the amount of rubbish in the sea and on the beaches.

Test yourself

Write a report of a field trip you made to the beach either with your class or with your parents.

1. What was the date of the trip? What beach did you go to?
2. How did you travel? How long did the journey take?
3. What plants (trees, grasses) and animals did you see on the way?
4. What plants did you see on the beach and in the sea?
   a) How far are the land plants from the sea?
   b) How are the plants different from plants at home or school?
5. What animals did you see on the beach and in the sea?
   a) How are the animals different from animals at home or at school?
   b) Do you think the animals that live in the sea can live on land? Why?
   c) Do you think the animals that live in the sea can live in fresh water? Why?
6. Draw two different animals you saw in the sea or on the beach. Write a sentence about each animal you draw.

(Performance assessment)

Chapter 13
Solid, Liquid, Gas

Classifying

Everything is made of **matter**. Matter can be in three different forms: solid, liquid and gas.

Activity 1 Solid, liquid, gas

Your group will need:
- a clean stone
- a tin lid e.g. a biscuit-tin lid
- a plastic container with some water in it
- an empty plastic container
- a clean drinking straw for each pupil

Safety!
- Do not use each other's straws.

1 Look at the stone carefully. Notice its shape.
2 Drop the stone on the tin lid. Observe what happens.
3 Is the stone still the same shape?
4 Pour a small amount of the water into the lid.

Share materials

5 Has the water changed shape?
6 Hold the empty container as if you were pouring water out of it into the lid.
7 What do you see? Was there anything in the container? Discuss with your group.

Objectives

At the end of the chapter pupils should be able to:
- demonstrate and state whether a substance is a solid, liquid or gas (pages 62–65).
- identify and name a substance as being a liquid, a solid or a gas (pages 65–66).

Classifying

8 Blow through your straw at the water. What do you see?
Let everyone in the group try this.

9 Hold your hand in front of the straw and blow.
What do you feel?

A stone is a **solid**.
A solid has a definite size and shape. It does not change its shape. It always takes up the same amount of space.

Water is a **liquid**.
A liquid always takes up the same amount of space. But it changes shape to fit the container it is in.

Air is a **gas**.
A gas fills any space it is put into. It can change its size and shape.

Most gases, like air, are invisible. You cannot see them. But you can feel them. When the wind blows you feel the air pushing against you. When you blew through the straw in Activity 1 you could feel the air. The air could push the water. **Oxygen**, **carbon dioxide** and **nitrogen** are some gases that make up air.

Do not confuse the gas you get at a gas station with gases like air! The gas used in cars is short for 'gasoline'. But gasoline is not a gas, it is a liquid!

Classifying

Activity 2 Liquids

Your group will need:
- a clear plastic jar or bottle partly filled with water
- an empty clear plastic jar, a different shape from the first one

1 Look carefully at the surface of the water in the bottle. What shape is it? Is it level?

2 Tilt the bottle slowly. What happens to the surface of the water?

3 Slowly pour the water into the empty jar. Watch the shape of the water as you are pouring it.

4 Look at the new shape of the water in the jar.

A liquid does not have a shape of its own. It takes the shape of the part of the container it occupies.

When liquid in a container is tilted, its surface is always level.

Activity 3 What about sand?

Your group will need:
- a clear plastic bottle or jar partly filled with sand
- an empty clear plastic jar, a different shape from the first one
- a hand lens

1 Look carefully at the sand in the bottle. Is the surface level?

2 Use the hand lens to look at the particles of sand. Observe their shape and size. Draw a sand particle.

Classifying

3 Pour the sand into the jar, as you did with the water in Activity 2.
Watch the shape of the sand as you pour it.

4 Look at the sand in the jar. Does it fill the shape of the new jar like the water did? Is the surface of the sand level?

5 Look at the particles of sand again with the hand lens. Have they changed size? Have they changed shape? Draw a sand particle again.

6 Is sand a solid or a liquid? What do you think?

Activity 4 Which is it?

Look at these objects. Which are solids? Which are liquids? Which are gases?

Classifying

Make a table like this in your notebook. The first one has been done for you.

Object	Solid	Liquid	Gas
book	✓		
oil			
air			

Summary
- Matter can be in three states: solid, liquid or gas.
- A solid has a definite shape and size.
- A liquid has a definite size, but it takes the shape of the container it is in.
- A gas changes shape and size to fill any container it is put in.

Test yourself

For each task, write down **A**, **B**, **C** or **D**.

1 Ryan poured a liquid from a glass into a jar. The liquid now

   A fills up the jar
   B keeps the same shape
   C has a larger volume
   D keeps the same volume

   (Objective 1)

2 Which of these is solid at room temperature?

   A air   **B** water   **C** steam   **D** fine sand

   (Objective 2)

3 Which of these is a gas at room temperature?

   A ice   **B** air   **C** plastic   **D** water

   (Objective 2)

Chapter 14

Classifying

Project Clean-up

When you eat a fruit, do you eat the skin? You usually throw away banana skins, orange skins and other fruit skins. Write down the names of five other things you throw away.

We call the bits we throw away **waste** or rubbish. Throwing away rubbish from homes, schools, stores and hospitals can create ugly sights. It can also be dangerous for people's health.

Activity 1 A survey of school waste

Your group will need:
- some newspaper
- gloves (or plastic bags that you can put over your hands and tie loosely at the wrists)
- 2 plastic garbage bags, one medium and one small
- twist ties

Safety!
- Wear gloves when handling rubbish.
- Wash your hands after this activity.

1 Discuss with your group what things pupils in your class throw away most. Here are some things you might think of:

Objective

At the end of this chapter pupils should be able to:
- identify and list types of items that make up solid waste found in and around the school grounds (pages 67–69).

67

Classifying

2. Write down what you agree would make:
   a) the biggest pile of rubbish
   b) the second largest pile of rubbish
   and so on.

3. Choose one member of your group to be in charge of the small garbage bag, and another to be in charge of the medium-size bag.

4. For 1 week, save all the rubbish you would normally throw away at school.
   Do not put it in the bin or throw it down in the school yard. Instead, put all food scraps, fruit skins and so on in the small garbage bag.
   Put all other garbage in the other bag.

5. Make sure the bag with the food scraps is kept tightly closed with a twist tie. Keep the bag away from animals.

6. At the end of the week (or before the food scraps begin to smell too much) empty the contents of the medium size bag onto a sheet of newspaper.
   (Remember to wear gloves.)

7. Sort the rubbish into different piles: tin cans, bottles, paper and so on.

8. You now have a bag full of food waste and several piles of other kinds of waste. Which kind of waste is there most of? Was the prediction you made in step 2 very good/good/not so good?

Tackling waste

You may have found waste materials that could be **re-used** or **recycled**. Jars and bottles can often be re-used, or the glass can be recycled to make new bottles.

If you found any waste like this, pass it on to people who can make use of it.

Classifying

Project

If your school yard has a lot of rubbish in it, you might like to clean it up. Wear gloves. Collect the waste in garbage bags. Do not pick up broken glass, empty pesticide bottles or tins, or corroded batteries. If you think something could be harmful to your health, tell your teacher. The teacher will arrange for its safe disposal.

Summary
- The rubbish we throw away is called waste.
- Waste is unsightly and can be dangerous to health.
- Solid waste can be glass, metal, paper, food scraps, fruit skins and so on.
- Keep the Caribbean beautiful.

Chapter 15 — Communicating
Life Cycles

Plants and animals produce young ones. The young ones grow and develop. They become adults. The adults produce more young ones. This is called the **life cycle** of that plant or animal.

A life cycle

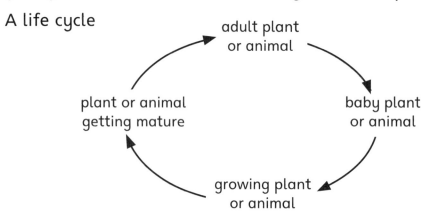

Insects

Insects lay eggs. The eggs hatch into young ones. Some young insects look like their parents, but are smaller. They change gradually into adult insects. Cockroaches are like this.

Insects have a hard outer covering that cannot grow bigger. So when the baby cockroach grows bigger its skin splits and falls off. This is called **moulting**. The cockroach has a new soft skin, which slowly hardens.

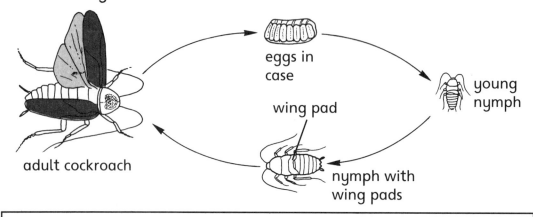

> **Objective**
> At the end of the chapter pupils should be able to:
> - describe the changes that insects, frogs and birds undergo as they grow and develop (pages 70–74).

Communicating

When the cockroach grows a bit bigger, it moults again. A cockroach may moult 13 times before it becomes an adult. The young cockroach is like a small adult but has no wings. It is called a **nymph**.

Some young insects do not look like their parents at all. They look like a different animal.

Butterflies lay eggs on the leaves of plants. The eggs hatch into tiny **larvae**. Butterfly larvae are called **caterpillars**. The caterpillars eat leaves. They moult several times as they grow.

The caterpillar stops eating and turns into a **pupa**. The pupa does not move about. But inside it is turning into a butterfly. At the right time, the pupa's outer skin splits open and an adult butterfly comes out.

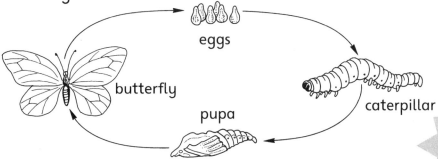

Respect and help each other

Activity 1   Keeping caterpillars

Your group will need:
- a clear plastic container with a lid
- a nail and hammer
- a leaf with butterfly eggs on it
- twigs and leaves from the plant the eggs came from
- a small jar of water

Safety!
- Be careful when using the nail.
- Ask an adult to help you.

1. Look at the underneath of leaves of lime, orange or other trees until you find one that has tiny butterfly eggs on it.
2. Carefully pick the twig with the leaf and put it in a small jar of water in your container. Add a few more twigs and leaves from the same kind of plant to the container.

Communicating

3 Use the nail to make holes in the lid of the container. The holes will let air get in. Put the lid on the container.

4 Put the container in a well-lit place, but not in direct sun. Look at it every day. Write down what you see happening.

5 When the caterpillars hatch they will eat the leaves. You will need to pick fresh leaves for them each day. Make sure they are the same kind of leaves that the eggs were on.

6 When the caterpillars are full grown they will turn into pupae. Watch the pupae every day. One day, if you are lucky, they will split open and a butterfly will emerge. What kind of butterflies did yours turn out to be?

Frogs

Frogs are animals that can live in water and on land. They are **amphibians**.

Frogs lay their eggs in water. Each egg is a blob of jelly with a black spot in the middle. The eggs are closely packed together and are called **frog spawn**.

The black spot in each egg grows into a head and a tail, and eventually a **tadpole** hatches out of the jelly. The tadpole grows a mouth, and gills to breathe with. It eats water plants.

As the tadpole grows bigger its feathery gills disappear. It grows a pair of hind legs. Then it grows a pair of front legs. Its tail gets shorter and shorter until it is completely absorbed. The tadpole has become a small frog.

Communicating

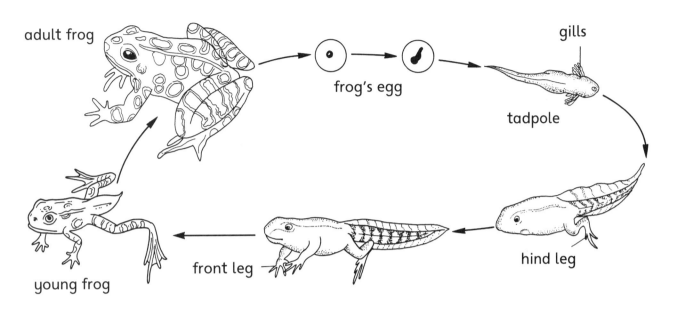

Activity 2 Keeping tadpoles

Your group will need:
- a large clear plastic container
- a jar to collect frog spawn in

Safety!
- Be careful not to fall into the water.
- An adult should go to the pond with you.

1 Find a pond or ditch that has frog spawn in it.

2 Fill the large container with water from the pond or ditch. Add some of the weeds from the pond, and some stones that have green stuff growing on them. Add one large stone that sticks up above the water.

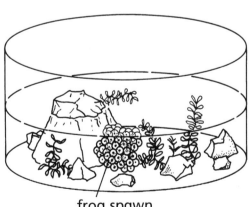

frog spawn

3 Carefully use your jar to scoop some frog spawn into the container.

4 Keep the container in a well-lit place, but not in direct sun. Look at it every day. Record what you observe. Add more pond water if you need to.

Communicating

5 You may need to collect some fresh plants for your tadpoles to eat. When they start to grow legs you can hang a small piece of meat in the water for them to eat. But be careful that the meat does not go bad. Adult frogs feed on insects.

6 When your tadpoles turn into frogs and start to climb out of the water, take them back to the pond or ditch where you found them.

Birds

Birds lay eggs too. Inside the egg is an **embryo** which will develop into a chick. The chick is attached to the yolk (the yellow part of the egg). The yolk is the chick's food. The white watery part of the egg gives the chick water. The chick gets air from an air space at the blunt end of the egg.

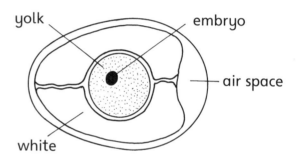

When the chick has grown to fill the egg, it cracks the egg shell and hatches out. Most baby birds have no feathers to start with, but chickens and ducklings have soft, fluffy down feathers. Ducks and fowls make their nests on the ground, so ducklings need to be able to run and swim as soon as they hatch, and chickens need to be able to run around.

The parent birds look after the chicks and feed them. After about five weeks the chicks have grown flight feathers and learn to fly. Birds become fully adult when they are about a year old. Fowls do not fly well.

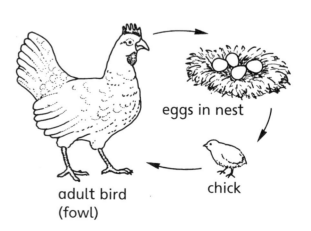

Communicating

Summary

- All living things have a life cycle: adult ⇄ young

- Insects, frogs and birds all lay eggs.
- In some insects (e.g. the cockroach, the grasshopper), the young look like small adults without wings. They moult as they grow bigger.
- In some insects the young do not look at all like the adults. Their eggs hatch into larvae. They turn into pupae. The pupae turn into the adults.
- Frogs lay eggs called frog spawn. These eggs hatch into tadpoles. The tadpoles gradually turn into adult frogs.
- Birds' eggs have yellow yolk which provides food for the developing chick. They also have a white part from which they get water and an air space.
- When some chicks hatch out of eggs they do not have feathers. Their parents must look after them until they can fly and feed themselves.

Test yourself

For each task, write down **A**, **B**, **C** or **D**.

1 Butterflies and moths develop in which order?

   A egg, pupa, larva (caterpillar), adult
   B adult, egg, pupa, larva (caterpillar)
   C adult, egg, larva (caterpillar), pupa, adult
   D egg, larva (caterpillar), pupa, adult

(Objective 1)

2 The locust, grasshopper and cockroach develop in which order?

   A adult, egg, adult   B egg, nymph, adult
   C egg, larva, nymph, adult   D egg, nymph, pupa, adult

(Objective 1)

Chapter 16 — Communicating

Bar Graphs

A **bar graph** is one way of showing information or data so that it is easy to understand.

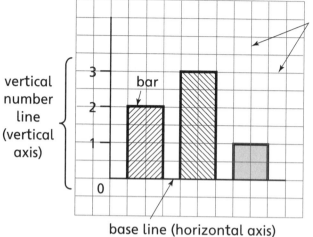

Here are some rules for drawing a bar graph:

- All bars in a graph must start at the same base line (horizontal axis).
- The numbers on the vertical number line correspond to the lines of the grid, not to the spaces between them.
- The base line is the 'zero' (0) level of the vertical number line.
- The vertical bars must be centred on the grid lines.
- The bars must be properly labelled and have a key.

Activity 1   A 'solid' bar graph

Your group will need:

- 13 blocks of the same size and shape: 4 yellow, 3 green, 6 white (these could be wooden blocks, or made from styrofoam trays stuck together)
- a sheet of graph paper for each pupil
- green and yellow crayons

Objectives

At the end of the chapter pupils should be able to:
- name units (numbers/objects) along the vertical and horizontal axes of a bar graph (pages 76–77).
- make a bar graph using numbers and objects (pages 77–78).
- distinguish between quantities shown on a bar graph in terms such as 'greater than', 'less than', 'greatest', 'least' (pages 78–79).

Communicating

1. Pile the blocks one on the other like this:

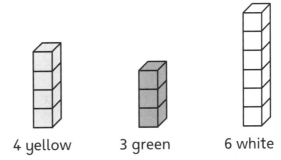

4 yellow   3 green   6 white

2. Draw a bar graph in your book like this: Colour the bars of your graph yellow, green and white.

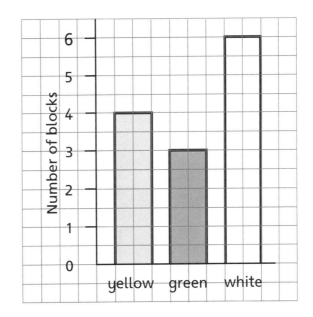

3. If you took the graph home and showed it to your parents, would they know how many yellow blocks are on your desk, even though they have not seen them? Write your answer as a sentence in your book.

Activity 2 Brothers and sisters

Your group will need:
- graph paper for each pupil

1. Your teacher will ask the class, 'How many pupils have no brothers or sisters?' When the pupils who have no brothers or sisters put up their hands, your teacher will count them and write the number on the board.

2. Now your teacher will count how many pupils have one brother or sister, then two and so on until all pupils have been counted.

Communicating

3 Your teacher will make a table on the board with these numbers. It might look like this one:

Number of brothers and sisters	0	1	2	3	4	5	6	7	8
Number of pupils	0	1	2	3	4	6	3	2	2

4 This is the graph that was drawn from the table above:

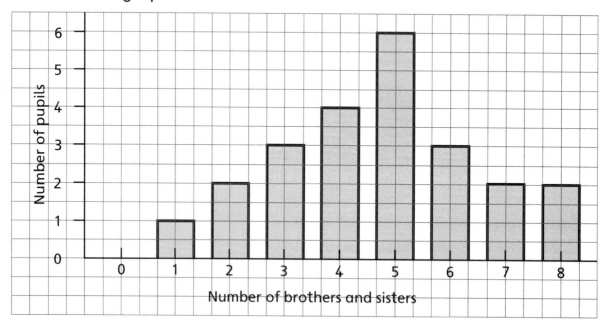

Now draw a graph like this, but use the table your teacher has made on the board.

5 Discuss the data table and your graph with your group. How many pupils in your class have no brothers or sisters? How many have fewer than three brothers and sisters? How many have more than six brothers and sisters?

6 What is the most common number of sisters and brothers? Are there more pupils with three sisters and brothers than with two?

It is easier to see the answers to some of these questions by looking at the bar graph than by looking at the table.

Communicating

Activity 3   Another bar graph

You will need:
- graph paper

Lucille decided to record the room temperature every day for a month. This table shows her results:

Temperature (°C) on horizontal axis	29	30	31	32	33	34	35
Number of days on vertical axis	2	3	10	13	1	0	2

1. Draw a bar graph of Lucille's results. Put the temperatures along the base line (horizontal axis). Put the numbers of days on the vertical number line (vertical axis).
2. What was the most common temperature that month?
3. How many days were hotter than usual?

Summary
- A bar graph is used to show information or data.
- You can compare things more easily on a bar graph than in a table.

Test yourself

1. Prepare a bar graph to show the number of rainy, cloudy and clear days for a week of your choice.
   Write the dates and make a key. Put this graph into your portfolio if you wish.

(Performance assessment)

Chapter 17
Food Chains

Communicating

Producers and consumers

Plants use energy from the sun to make their own food. Plants are called **producers**.

Some animals eat plants. Some animals eat other animals. Animals are **consumers**.

Activity 1   Animals that eat plants

Your group will need:
- some plastic animals: cow, rabbit, horse

1. Place the plastic animals on your desk. Imagine they are hungry.
2. Go outside and get some food for each animal.
3. What did you give the horse to eat? What did you give the rabbit and the cow?
4. Look at these pictures:

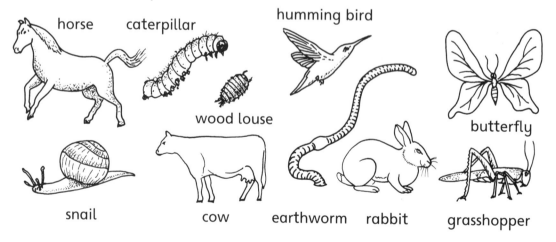

Objectives

At the end of the chapter pupils should be able to:
- identify animals that feed on plants (page 80).
- identify animals that feed on other animals (page 81).
- construct a food chain (page 82).

80

Communicating

5 Make a list in your book of all these animals and add the food they eat.

Write your list like this:

grass → cow

The arrow means 'is eaten by'.

Activity 2 Animals that eat other animals

1 Look at these pictures:

2 Discuss with your group which of these animals eat other animals.

3 Write the animals in pairs like this:

grasshopper → praying mantis

The arrow means that the praying mantis eats the grasshopper.

Communicating

Food chains

Often a plant is eaten by an animal. Then the animal is eaten by another animal. Here is an example:

grass → rabbit → dog

This is called a **food chain**.

Activity 3   Food chains

1 Here is a small pond:

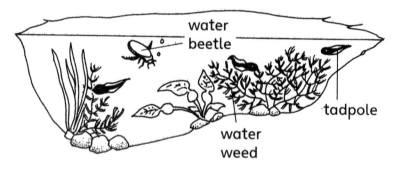

Discuss with your group what will happen in it.
Copy and complete this food chain:

water weed → ? → ?

2 Discuss with your group what a caterpillar eats.
What eats a caterpillar?
Copy and complete this food chain:

? → caterpillar → ?

3 Make another food chain with a shark.

4 Study this food chain:

plant → bee → human

Does the bee eat the plant?
Does the human eat the bee?
Explain the food chain.

Communicating

Summary
- Plants make their own food. They are called producers.
- Some animals eat plants. Some animals eat other animals. They are called consumers.
- When a plant is eaten by an animal and the animal is eaten by another animal, this is called a food chain.
- A food chain very often begins with a plant.

Test yourself

For each task write down **A**, **B**, **C** or **D**.

Use these food chains to answer tasks 1 and 2.

plants → rabbit → fox
plants → squirrel → hawk
plants → snail → bird → cat

1. In the food chains above, the animals that feed on plants only are

   A rabbit, snail, bird
   B cat, snail, fox
   C snail, rabbit, squirrel
   D snail, fox, hawk

   (Objective 1)

2. In the food chains above, the animals that feed on animals only are

   A cat, fox, rabbit, hawk
   B hawk, fox, bird, cat
   C cat, hawk, snail, fox
   D rabbit, squirrel, snail, bird

   (Objective 2)

3. Which one of the following makes a food chain?

   A bush → bee → bird → hawk
   B bee → bird → hawk → bush
   C bush ← bee ← bird ← hawk
   D hawk → bush → bee → bird

   (Objective 3)

83

Chapter 18 — Communicating

Which Aeroplane Flies Best?

Activity 1 Making a model aeroplane

Your group will need:

- a sheet of paper for each pupil

Here are instructions for making a paper aeroplane:

1 Fold

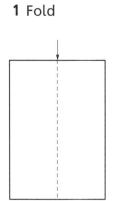

2 Fold in half along dotted line

3 Fold in corners

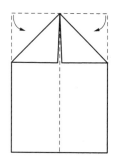

4 Fold in along dotted lines to centre line

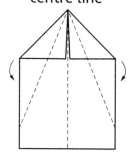

5 Fold in half along centre line

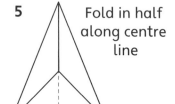

6 Bend wings down along dotted lines

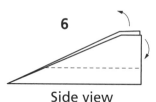

Side view

7

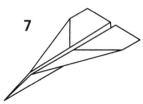

Some possible modifications

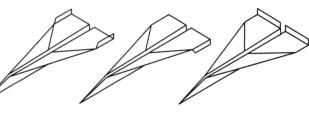

1 Discuss the design of this aeroplane with your group.

Objectives

At the end of the chapter the pupils should be able to:
- demonstrate a procedure for making a model aeroplane (pages 84–85).
- redesign or alter the aeroplane to improve the time it stays up in the air or the distance it flies (pages 85–86).
- write a report on the construction details of the improved model (pages 86–87).

Communicating

2. Each member of the group can make changes to the design to improve the way it flies. You might change the shape of the sheet of paper you start with, or fold it differently, or bend the wings differently. Write down the changes you are going to make.

Contribute ideas

3. Make your own aeroplane, the way you have designed it.

4. Try out your aeroplane. Make any improvements that will help it to fly further.

5. When you are happy with your aeroplane, write your name, your group's name and the name of the aeroplane on the model.

Activity 2 Launching

Your group will need:
- the aeroplanes you made in Activity 1
- chalk

1. Find a large clear space in the classroom or the school yard.

2. Take turns to try your aeroplanes. Throw the aeroplane up and forward. Use the chalk to mark where it lands.

3. Throw your aeroplane three times. Leave the furthest chalk mark and rub out the others. Write your name beside the mark.

Communicating

4 When everyone in your group has launched their aeroplane three times, look at the chalk marks. Whose aeroplane flew furthest?

5 Look at the aeroplane that flew furthest. Discuss it in your group. Can you improve it even more?

Activity 3 Inter-group aeroplane competition

Your group will need:
- your group's winning aeroplane
- measuring tape
- chalk

1 Choose one member of your group to launch your aeroplane.

2 Throw each of the aeroplanes three times and mark the furthest distance, as you did in Activity 2.

3 Which aeroplane flew furthest? Use the measuring tape to measure how many metres the winner flew.

Project

The Douglass Paper Aeroplane Corporation chose you as the Chief of Design for the Douglass Paper Aeroplane Team. The corporation wants to win the paper aeroplane event in the Olympics, for the longest flight distance. It also wants to break the world record of 4.8 metres. This record was established by the Boeing in 1986.

You have to write a report on how you would design the corporation's aeroplane for the competition. You must state all the things that affect a paper aeroplane's flight. Using what you learnt in Activity 2, write six or more sentences to describe what you would do to win the Olympic competition.

First, write a rough copy. Discuss it with your group. Revise it and make a final copy. Show it to your teacher.

Communicating

Summary
- You can improve how a paper aeroplane flies by making changes to the design, trying it out and making further changes.

Test yourself

1 First follow steps **1** to **7** on page 84.

2 To make the tail, cut about 3 cm from the end vertically up.

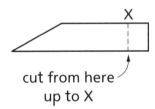

Note that the wings are not shown here.

3 Push up the cut piece from below and press the fold flat.

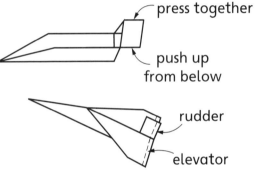

1 The diagram above shows how to make a paper plane with a rudder and elevators. The rudder makes the plane turn and the elevators can make it loop up or down. Make the plane and fly it. Using the rudder, try to make it turn to the right and to the left. Use the elevators to loop it up and down. You may use glue or paper clips to improve it.

Write a short report on how you would show your plane's turning and looping actions, and what you can do to improve these actions.

(Performance assessment)

Chapter 19

Inferring

Concealed Objects

Someone places a package on a dry table. After a few minutes the package and the table top become wet.

We **observe** the wetness. We may make several **inferences**:

(1) There is a liquid in the package.

(2) A container with liquid in the package has broken.

(3) Someone may have dropped the package.

We are *certain* that the package and the table are wet – we observed this with our eyes.

We are *not so certain* when we infer that someone dropped the package, or that the package contains a bottle of liquid that broke.

When we make an inference we try to explain what we observe. We try to give reasons for what we observe. If you want to make a reasonable inference you must make many observations. It is better to make an inference after several observations than to make a lucky 'correct' guess. Being 'right' when you make an inference means stating *why* you have inferred that from your observations.

> **Objective**
> At the end of the chapter pupils should be able to:
> - make inferences from observations about concealed objects (page 89).

Inferring

Activity 1 Better than a guess!

Your group will need:
- a scarf to use as a blindfold
- a box containing a variety of objects; for example, soap, an onion, a pencil, a marble, a ball, a peppermint, a string of beads, a ball of plasticine, a plastic animal, a glove and so on

Safety!
- Do not try to taste any of the objects.
- Do not put your nose too close when you are smelling things.

1. Blindfold each member of your group in turn.
2. Pick one of the objects out of the box and give it to the blindfolded pupil.
3. The blindfolded person must try to infer what she or he is holding. You cannot use the sense of taste or sight, but you can use touch, smell and hearing.
4. When you think you know what the object is, tell the rest of the group and say why you infer that.
5. Write your answer in your book like this:

   'I inferred that the object was _____ because _____.

6. Repeat the process until every group member gets a chance to make an inference.

Summary
- You can observe some things directly.
- You can make inferences about things that you cannot observe directly.
- The more observations you make first, the better your inference is likely to be.

Chapter 20 — Using Graphs

Predicting

In many science experiments you will collect **data**. Data is information about things. It is usually given as numbers.

Graphs are a useful way to show data. They make it easier to see what the data means. You can also use graphs to make **predictions** about things.

Activity 1 Are you a square?

Your group will need:
- a metre rule or metric tape measure
- graph paper for each pupil

1 Work in pairs. Get your partner to measure your height and your arm-span (in centimetres).

Write down your measurements.
Now measure your partner's height and arm-span.

2 Look at these pictures:

square

height almost equal to arm-span (difference less than 3 centimetres)

tall rectangle

height greater than arm-span (by more than 3 centimetres)

wide rectangle

height less than arm-span (by more than 3 centimetres)

Which one are you?

Objectives

At the end of the chapter pupils should be able to:
- make predictions based on data presented on a bar graph (pages 91–92).
- test the predictions (pages 92–93).

Predicting

3 Make a table like this for your group:

Name	Height (cm)	Arm-span (cm)	Square	Tall rectangle	Wide rectangle
Ali	120	114		✓	

4 Count how many of each shape there are in your group.

5 Your teacher will ask each group how many of each shape they have. He or she will write on the board how many of each shape there are in the whole class.

6 Use the numbers for the class to make a bar graph. First draw a horizontal axis (number line) and a vertical axis like this:

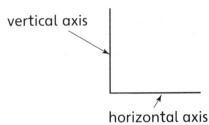

7 Along the **horizontal axis** write 'Square', 'Tall rectangle' and 'Wide rectangle'.
Along the **vertical axis** write 'Number of pupils'.

8 Draw three bars to show the numbers for your class.

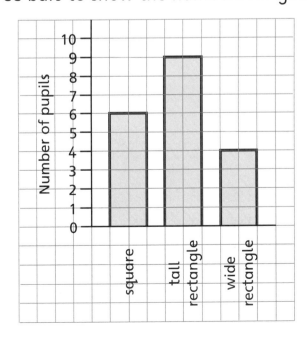

Predicting

9. What shape are most pupils in your class? What shape are the fewest pupils?

10. If a new pupil came into the class, what shape do you predict that the new pupil will be?

11. Ask your teacher to 'borrow' any pupil from another standard 2 class. Measure that pupil's height and arm-span.

12. What shape is the new pupil?

13. Was your prediction *very good* or *not so good*?

> Give praise to others

Activity 2 Peas in a pod

Your group will need:
- 26 pea pods or Barbados pride pods

Safety!
- Wash your hands after this activity.
- Do not put the peas into your mouth.

1. Open each pod. Count the number of peas in it. Record your data in a table like this:

Number of peas in pod	Score	Total
1		0
2	.	0
3	✓	1
4	✓✓✓✓✓✓✓✓✓ ✓✓✓✓✓✓	17
5	✓✓✓✓✓✓✓✓✓✓	10
6	✓✓	2

For example, there was 1 pod with 3 peas and 17 pods with 4 peas in my bunch of 30 pea pods.

Predicting

2. Use your data to draw a bar graph. On the horizontal axis put 'Number of peas'. On the vertical axis put 'Number of pods'.

3. Discuss your graph with your group.
   What was the largest number of peas in a pod?
   How many pods had the largest number of peas?
   What was the smallest number of peas in a pod?
   How many pods had the smallest number of peas?

   What was the number of peas that you found most often?

4. Get another pod. Predict how many peas there will be.

5. Open the pod. How many peas are there? Was your prediction *good* or *not so good*?

> **Summary**
> - Graphs can show data in a useful way.
> - You can predict things by studying the pattern of a graph.

Test yourself

For this task, write down **A, B, C** or **D**.

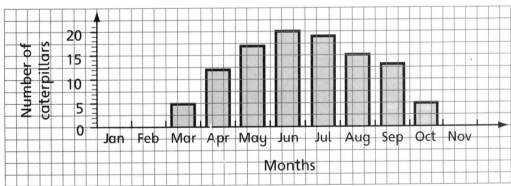

1. The graph above shows the number of caterpillars which Nicky caught from January to November. You could predict that the number of caterpillars Nicky would catch in December would be

   A 0   B 5   C 14   D 20

(Objective 1)

93

Revision Test

1 Clouds form when water vapour rises and

   A gets too heavy
   B cools on cold surfaces of tiny dust particles
   C thunder rolls
   D tiny drops of water form on the outside of a glass

2 In order to grow healthy a plant must have

   A air, water and light   B soil, water and plant food
   C fertilizer, water and soil D plant food, soil and good care

3 Sintra did not go to school today. She has a fever. Which letter shows Sintra's body temperature?

   A 105°C   B 40°C   C 98°C   D 102°C

4 The spring balances opposite are all graduated in force units.
   The object that weighs the most is

   A   B   C   D
   Give a reason for your choice.

5 Michael has 20 items each of sizes shown in the diagram below. He wishes to use the four sieves to separate them. He should arrange the sieves in the order shown at

   A 2 3 4 1   B 1 3 4 2   C 3 1 4 2   D 2 4 1 3

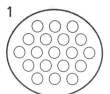 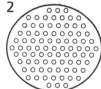 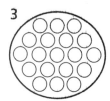 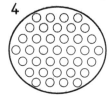 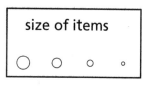

6 A piece of wood of mass 60 grams floats in water. A piece of iron of mass 40 grams sinks in water. This happens because sinking and floating depend on the

   A mass of the object   B size of the object
   C amount of water in the   D material of the object
     container

Revision Test

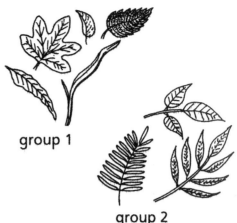

group 1

group 2

7 The leaves are grouped into

- A jagged-edged leaves and smooth-edged leaves
- B simple leaves and compound leaves
- C thin-bladed leaves and broad leaves
- D large leaves and small leaves

8 Some plants living near the seaside have thick leaves. They store water in their leaves because

- A not much fresh water is available
- B they take in lots of sea water
- C their roots run down into the sea
- D the waves splash water on them

9 The order of development of the frog is

- A 1, 2, 3, 4, 5
- B 4, 5, 2, 1, 3
- C 3, 1, 2, 4, 5
- D 4, 1, 5, 2, 3

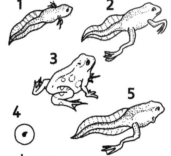

10 Marian has a box with four cubes and one sphere. Harry's box has five spheres and nine cones. The graph that shows what Marian has in her box is

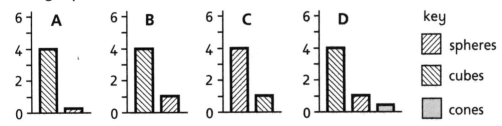

11 Which of the following diagrams represents a food chain?

- A grass – grasshopper – toad – snake – hawk
- B hawk → snake → toad → grasshopper → grass
- C grass → grasshopper → toad → snake → hawk
- D grasshopper → grass → toad → hawk → snake

95

Revision Test

12 The graph shows the level of water in a 100 ml graduated cylinder as marbles are added. The water level when 25 marbles are added will be

A 50 ml   B 60 ml
C 70 ml   D 80 ml

Say what information you used to make your prediction.

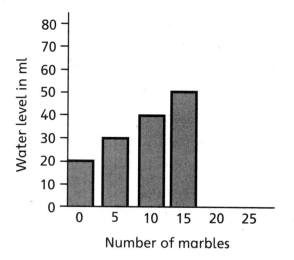

Glossary

carbon dioxide   a gas in the atmosphere; it is made by plants in the food making process (page 63)

caterpillar   larva of the butterfly or moth (page 71)

components   parts (page 39)

down feathers   the small fluffy feathers that cover the body of young birds (page 74)

embryo   the developing organism during the early stages (page 74)

life cycle   stages in an organism's life from the fertilised egg in one generation to the fertilised egg in the next (page 70)

moulting   shedding the outer layer of skin, feathers or exoskeleton (page 70)

nitrogen   one of the gases in the atmosphere (page 63)

oxygen   a gas in the atmosphere that is necessary for breathing and burning (page 63)

precipitation   release of water from the atmosphere in the form of rain or snow (page 6)

yolk   the yellow part of the egg used as food for the developing embryo (page 74)

96